MW01442090

Different Me, Different Us

The readable part of couples therapy

By Maddie Hundley, MMFT, LMFT

Published by Zillennial Therapy

DIFFERENT ME, DIFFERENT US
Copyright © 2024 by Maddie Hundley

All rights reserved. No part of this book may be reproduced in any form without permission in writing from the publisher, except by a reviewer who may quote brief passages in a review.

ISBN: [9798884820876]

First Edition: 2024

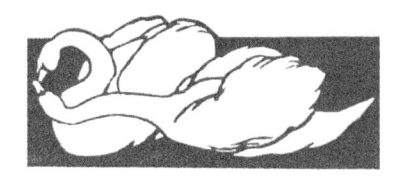

DEDICATION

To Jared, my husband, best friend, and partner for life; Thank you for allowing me to try so much of this book out on you, but also for supporting me through everything life has and will throw at us.

You are my favorite part of my story.

ACKNOWLEDGEMENTS

I would like to thank the following people for their support throughout the process of writing this book.

    Jared Hundley
    Phillipa Vaporciyan
    Anya Vaporciyan
    Zoe Carlson-Stadler

Editor in Chief
    Francesca Nardi

Illustrator
    Rachel Fritts

Research & Inclusivity Manager
    Ally Coulton

I would like to thank my wonderful 2024 interns, who helped me complete this book on time.

    Paola Ruiz
    Maggie Bird
    Francesca Nardi
    Ally Coulton
    Bertha Rios-Neikirk

Other thanks to:

    Alex Whitman, MA
    Taylor Spaziani, MA, MFTC, LPCC
    Daniel Williamson, MFT-A
    Dr. Michael Grey, PsyD, LMFT, ABS
    Allison Marx, LMFT, ATR
    Madison Jones, BSECE
    Aubrey McWilliams
    Rachel Sparks
    Gabriel Cooper MS, LMFT

TABLE OF CONTENTS

No More Gatekeeping............................... **18**
    Your Roadmap.................................21
    A Little About Me............................ 22
    The "Perfect Relationship".................... 25
    So, why therapy, or why did you pick up this book?.. 33
    Your Narrative............................... 36
    Your Table of Contents: Your Stories.......... 38

Emotional Connection & Communication............... **44**
    Love Languages............................... 45
    Emotional Safety............................. 50
    Attachment & Intimacy........................ 52
    Core Negative Beliefs Challenged in Arguments.. 56
        Attachment Styles and Related Beliefs........58
        Fears and Beliefs in Relationships...........60
        Core Negative Beliefs in Relationships.......61
    Apology & Repair............................. 71
        Apology Languages............................73
    Essential Phrases for Mending Conflict:....... 77
    ACE Scores Test.............................. 79
    Our History Informs Our Now................... 82
    Our Nervous System & Polyvagal Theory......... 84
    Moving into a State of Action................. 87

Sex, Pleasure, & Intimacy.......................... **89**
    The Importance of Intimacy................... 90
    Why Sex Gets Harder the Longer You're Together. 94
    Sex Therapy.................................. 97
    How Sexuality Works.......................... 99
        The Dual Control Model......................101
        Responsive Desire...........................104
        Hormones....................................108

    Fantasy & Desire............................112
    Sexual Blueprints..........................114
Sexual Trauma................................ 116
Self-Love..................................... 119
The Stopwatch Game............................ 124
Our Analogous Bodies.......................... 125
Challenges with Orgasm........................ 131
    For the Vulva..............................132
    For the Penis..............................135
Opening Up.................................... 137
Evolving Together Sexually.................... 139
Aftercare..................................... 141
Maintaining a Satisfying Sex Life in Long-Term Relationships:................................ 142
Should Y'all Go to Couples Therapy?........... 145
Appendix - Now What?.......................... 149
    What to Consider When Looking for a Couple's Therapist..................................150
    To Use Insurance or Not....................153
    Modalities You Can Choose From.............156
Directories: The Yellow Pages of Therapists... 158

CITATIONS................................... 161

PREFACE

This book was inspired by the collection of information I have gathered since I began studying relationships and sexuality in my early 20s and my own application of those ideas. Since then, I have been practicing as a couple's therapist focused on intimacy in Los Angeles, California, and now I am back in Austin, Texas, after a five-year hiatus. I am excited to present *Different Me, Different Us* to readers who want to learn about partnerships and how to thrive in them.

-Maddie Hundley (Sheffer), MMFT

FOREWORD

A strong, long-lasting romantic connection with another individual is a bond that many people seek to obtain in their lives. Relationships are the foundational cornerstone through which physical, emotional, and intellectual connections can be strengthened to create deep, sustained feelings of attachment with their partner(s).

In the search for that connection, many individuals are left with questions regarding intimacy, love, and how to build a powerful, meaningful, and significant connection with someone they love.

While the importance of therapy cannot be understated, and the fact that finding a therapist who you truly connect with can be one of the single most significant connections an individual can build, it is important to understand that therapy is most effective when one learns to *apply* the information they receive and *how* to apply it.

The relationship-empowering psychoeducation, information, and material taught to therapists that can truly benefit people and their relationships should be accessible to any who wish to obtain it, regardless of whether or not that individual or couple is able to financially afford the bill of therapy itself.

This book is the product of the labor of compiling pages upon pages of undergraduate and graduate degree notes and thousands of hours spent with clients, specifically focusing on their relationships and how to build intimacy, connection, trust, and love; it is the product of feeling that anyone should have readily available information to the methods and practices that can foster incredibly fulfilling romantic and sexual relationships with your partner; and it is the product of the realization that small, incremental, easy changes to the way you perceive yourself, your partner(s), and relationships can be the key to creating and achieving the relationship you have always wanted.

"Cogito, ergo sum,"
"I think, therefore I am"

-**René Descartes**

No More Gatekeeping

This book is a blend of my personal journey and professional insights, a combination shaped by my own experiences in love and marriage, alongside my work as a marriage & family therapist. Since 2016, my husband and I have been on a path filled with its own set of highs and lows, much like any couple out there. Just over a year ago, we decided to deepen our commitment and get married, a step that has only further enriched our understanding of what it means to share a life together.

This book isn't borne out of an ivory tower of academic theory but from real, lived experiences and the practical application of therapeutic principles that I have seen in my work with clients. I am passionate about breaking down the barriers that often keep essential relationship wisdom locked away in textbooks and therapy sessions, thus making it accessible to everyone.

My goal as I wrote this book was to help you and your partner develop the tools and understanding necessary to navigate the complexities of your relationship without having to be in weekly couples therapy. Or, maybe you are in couples therapy now, and your therapist suggested you read this book! This book can work in conjunction with therapy for those who want to learn more. Through it, you will enhance your communication and intimacy, learning to recognize and work through the challenges that inevitably arise when two lives intertwine.

Hopefully by sharing insights from my professional expertise and personal experiences, this book will create a space where academic knowledge and therapeutic insights become more relatable and accessible. It's designed to serve as a primer, similar to the understanding I've seen develop among couples in therapy along the way.

This book is for those wanting to strengthen their bond with each other not just addressing issues as they come up but laying a groundwork to prevent them from happening in the first place. It's an invitation to explore together, to learn and grow, and to create a relationship that stands the test of time and is filled with understanding, respect, and love.

Couples therapy is a phrase that might evoke a range of emotions, from hope and curiosity to apprehension and uncertainty. The truth is, seeking help for your relationship can be one of the bravest and most loving decisions you can make. It's a recognition that your relationship is worth investing in, and that you're willing to do the work to strengthen and nurture it.

However, the decision to seek couples therapy isn't always as straightforward as just Googling "therapist". For many people there are mental, physical, financial, and cultural barriers. Finances, for instance, can be a significant concern: traditional therapy sessions can come with a hefty price tag, making it inaccessible for many couples. Insurance is complicated to navigate, and it is often difficult to know where to start. Likewise, finding the time to attend sessions amidst busy work schedules, family commitments, and other responsibilities can feel like an uphill battle.

I would still encourage you to find your own couples therapy journey with a licensed clinician in your state, but if you are still deciding, in the meantime, you can read this book. Unlike traditional therapy, this book offers a flexible, accessible alternative that you can engage with at your own pace and in the comfort of your own home. You have the freedom to explore the insights, strategies, and practical tools offered within these pages on your own terms.

If you want to start your own couples therapy journey with a licensed clinician in your state, go to the appendix of this book to learn how to find a therapist that will be the right fit for you, how much to expect to pay, the pros and cons of using insurance, and more detailed information about the different styles of therapy. content is designed to assist you throughout your therapy journey by providing topics and valuable insights to enrich your conversations during sessions.

My hope is that this book will empower you and give you a significant advantage to put the power back in your hands, equipping you with the knowledge and skills you need to navigate the complexities of your relationship with confidence and intention. It's not about relying on a therapist to "fix" your relationship; it's about empowering you to be the architects of your own love story.

In this book, I will be using terms like "you" because I, too, am a human in a relationship, sharing these experiences just like everyone else. My personal experiences and education shape the narrative of this book, and I hope that through these stories and insights, you learn something valuable and grow to love yourself more.

Even if you are reading this book on your own because you want your relationship to be better, hopefully, you will bring what you learn into your relationship. It's a valuable resource for you if you are ready to start on your journey of self-discovery and relational growth. This book provides practical tools, insights, and exercises to support you every step of the way.

Your Roadmap

You will first read about the foundational elements of a relationship. Specifically, how to understand and communicate your emotions in order to maintain safety in your relationship. This will give you the tools to understand how you as an individual protect yourself and give you the words to communicate your feelings to get reassurance or forgiveness in your relationship. The second section of this book focuses on developing the sexual intimacy of your relationship. This section will walk you through why intimacy is important, how sexuality works, and how to improve your sex life in your relationship. Although this book will give you the foundational elements for your own DIY journey (or in conjunction with your own therapy journey), you will then come across a section solely dedicated to helping you, if you wish, find a couples therapist that will support you as your relationship continues to grow and evolve.

So, if you've ever felt hesitant about seeking couples therapy due to barriers like finances, time constraints, or even uncertainty about where to start, know that you're not alone. And know that there is another option—a path forward that is accessible, empowering, and filled with the potential for growth and transformation.

A Little About Me

I'm grateful to have earned my undergraduate degree in Psychology from St. Edward's University and my Master's degree in Marriage and Family Therapy from the University of Southern California (USC). After I finished grad school, I stayed in West Hollywood in Los Angeles, California for a few years until I finished my clinical hours and headed back to Austin, Texas, the same place I went to college and met my husband. I have had the privilege of working with diverse couples and individuals from all over California since then, with a variety of concerns, identities, and personalities, but the most rewarding has been the work I have done with couples surrounding intimacy.

I gained a strong foundation in therapeutic approaches and interventions during my time at USC, which I have subsequently combined with practical experience and further professional growth. As a mostly now online telehealth practitioner (usually wearing comfy pants), I've been able to witness up close the unique challenges and opportunities that come with navigating relationships in a dynamic modern world. I'm excited to share the knowledge and techniques I've gained from my training and experience, providing you with useful advice on how to build stronger ties and happier, more satisfying relationships.

Navigating the terrain of married life has been an interesting journey of self-discovery for me. I thought that all those years of dating would prepare me for the change, but I faced unexpected obstacles that changed the way I thought about marriage. I struggled with concepts like autonomy and fully sharing all of my life with someone, for better or worse.

Despite my background as a couples therapist, my relationship isn't immune to the occasional argument of misunderstanding. Whether it's bickering about the dishes (it's never about the dishes) or having the same disagreement for the hundredth time, my relationship is no different than yours or your neighbors. These types of arguments highlight the universality and complexity of relationship dynamics and our need for practical, actionable guidance.

One of the most unexpected hurdles was the process of changing my name. While I anticipated the joy of sharing a family name, the reality of redefining my identity has been overwhelming. Moving from Maddie Sheffer to Maddie Hundley has led me to reflect on who I am as I navigate the merging of my past and current selves.

Now fully embracing my new name, I find a sense of familiarity and empowerment in its resonance. With each utterance, it's a reminder of my commitment to my husband and our shared journey. The process of integrating this new identity is a period of transition, where echoes of my past mingle with the promise of our future.

Embracing Maddie Hundley as my new identity signifies more than a mere change in name; it symbolizes a move toward embracing my role as a partner and creating a shared life. Relationships are like mirrors that reflect both our inner and outside landscapes, as I've learned to realize while traveling this path. Specifically, marriage has developed into a potent self-reflection instrument that has helped me see facets of my identity that I had previously been blind to. Even if there are obstacles along the way, I'm seizing the chance to learn more about who I am and how I interact with other people.

I'm learning to embrace the discomfort of growth and change. Each day brings new revelations and insights, shaping my understanding of myself and my place in the world. As I fully embrace myself and all that I represent, I do so with a sense of anticipation and curiosity, eager to continue this journey of self-discovery within the context of my marriage.

The "Perfect Relationship"

When I entered my relationship with my husband, I had bought into the myths of the perfect relationship. But when I noticed the inevitable conflicts, I was caught off guard. Each argument left me feeling distraught, questioning whether it was a sign of something irreparably wrong. I couldn't comprehend how fighting could be healthy; it seemed counterintuitive, even absurd. However, as time passed and I pursued my studies in grad school, learning about the intricacies of relationship dynamics, I underwent a significant transformation. I came to understand that it wasn't the number of arguments or the severity of the conflict that mattered most—it was how we repaired those arguments. This realization was the key to unlocking the secrets of successful relationships. And the wonderful news? It's a skill that can be learned, practiced, and perfected—no matter where you find yourself on your relationship journey.

Dr. John and Dr. Julie Gottman, eminent figures in relationship psychology, have revolutionized our understanding of romantic partnerships. We will discuss multiple aspects of their research in this book.

Through their collaborative research, they've uncovered how trust, betrayal, repair, and conflict affect relationships, providing invaluable insights to the field. Their approach involved keen observation of couples' interactions over time, identifying key markers of relationship health such as communication styles and emotional responsiveness. They were the ones that discovered that repair is the most important factor in couples staying together. By emphasizing the bidirectional nature of relationships and the importance of positive interactions, the Gottmans offer practical tools that help navigate the challenges of intimacy and that have inspired part of this book.

Their work has shed light on the critical role of trust in relationships, has shattered myths, and provided evidence-based strategies for navigating the complexities of love and partnership. It's important to note, they acknowledge modern relationships' diversity, but their research was conducted with monogamous constructs in mind (J Gottman J. S. Gottman, 2015).

It is also important to highlight that their research can be adapted to diverse relationships. However, as a therapist who works with sexual and gender minorities, including folx who are polyamorous, this is not always our first approach. People within diverse constructs are often left out of the research because many concepts are rooted in monogamy.

According to the Gottmans, conflict in a relationship is not inherently detrimental; it's how you manage and repair that conflict that truly matters. Through their extensive observations of couples in both conflict and harmony, they identified key predictors of relationship satisfaction and longevity, which they call 'The Four Horsemen of the Apocalypse', helping people identify and address negative patterns in their relationship. The Gottmans also spoke on the concept of bids for connection and turning towards each other instead of away. They highlight the importance of effective communication, emotional attunement, and intentional acts of kindness in fostering lasting love.

The Four Horsemen of the Apocalypse—criticism, contempt, defensiveness, and stonewalling—have shown to be powerful predictors of relationship breakdown. These destructive communication patterns can severely damage a relationship, eroding trust, intimacy, and connection. Criticism attacks a person's character instead of addressing specific behaviors; contempt displays superiority and disdain toward a partner; defensiveness, though a natural reaction to feeling attacked or misunderstood, can escalate conflicts by shutting down communication; and stonewalling involves withdrawing from interactions and emotionally shutting down, cutting off any chance of resolution. Understanding and recognizing these toxic patterns is crucial for navigating arguments and repairing conflicts in relationships. By learning to identify and address the Four Horsemen, couples can cultivate healthier communication habits and build a stronger foundation for lasting love by identifying and addressing negative patterns.

THE FOUR HORSEMEN

Criticism
"You are so selfish"

"You are untrustworthy"

"You can't do anything right!"

Contempt
"How did I get stuck with such a loser?"

"I am too good for you"

Defensiveness
"Our issues are NOT my fault!"

They are all because of you"

"I'm too detached? At least, I don't need reassurance 24/7!"

Stonewalling
"I'm giving the silent treatment until they realize what they did wrong"

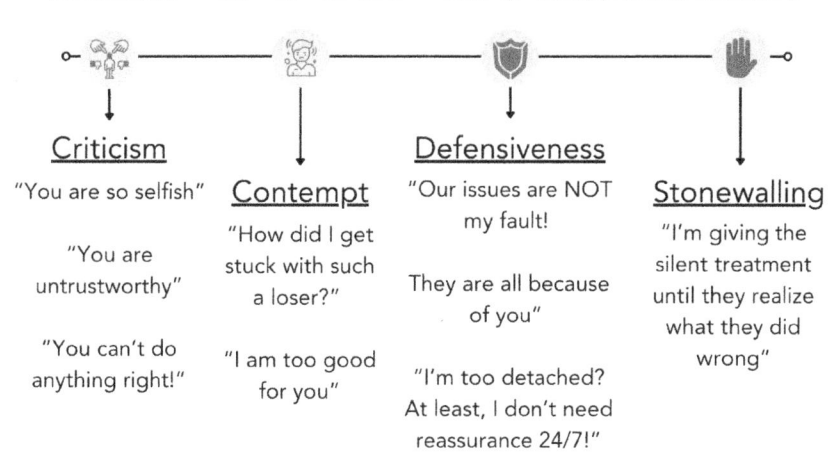

Bids for connection are invitations for communication and interactioncan. They take all sorts of forms, such as a question, a comment, a gesture, or a facial expression. These bids are subtle or overt attempts individuals make to connect emotionally with their partners. For example, a partner might share a personal story, express affection, or seek validation through a question or comment. These are incredibly important.

Recognizing and responding positively to these bids is crucial for fostering emotional intimacy and strengthening the bond between partners. When one partner makes a bid for connection, they are essentially reaching out for support, affirmation, or engagement. How the other partner responds to these bids—whether they acknowledge, ignore, or dismiss them—greatly influences the quality of the relationship. Couples who consistently respond to each other's bids with attentiveness, empathy, and warmth tend to experience greater satisfaction and closeness in their relationship.

Social work professor Brené Brown, like me, is from Houston. She is known for her influential TED talk on vulnerability and her extensive work on courage, shame, and empathy. Her research focuses on how shame can seriously interfere with our ability to form genuine connections. She started her research out by exploring the ins and outs of human relationships but quickly hit the wall of shame—that gnawing fear that we are somehow not enough and that if people really saw us, they'd turn away.

After six years of digging into the topic, talking to thousands, and running heaps of focus groups, Brené cracked the code: feeling worthy of love and belonging makes all the difference. She spotlights a group she calls "the wholehearted" folks who just get that they deserve love and belonging and live their lives embracing that truth. These wholehearted souls share a few game-changing traits:

```
"They dare to be imperfect, they're kind to
themselves (and others), and they don't shy
away from vulnerability."
```

Brené redefines vulnerability, showing it's not about weakness but about having the guts to face uncertainty, take risks, and open up emotionally.

Wrestling with your own vulnerability can lead to a major shift in how you see the world. Gratitude and joy are antidotes to fear and uncertainty, urging us to accept that we're enough as we are and to tune into that quiet voice inside that reassures us of our worthiness of love and connection.

In my practice, I integrate these ideas within a narrative approach. This kind of therapy seeks to help couples in pursuit of deepening their understanding of their relationship dynamics. Narrative therapy emphasizes the power of storytelling in shaping our perceptions and experiences, viewing individuals and relationships as stories as evolving stories. At the outset of therapy, I guide couples through an exercise designed to help them articulate their unique narrative—the story of their relationship. This exercise serves as a foundation for our work together, providing insight into each partner's perspective, values, and aspirations. (I will share an activity in a couple of sections).

Throughout our sessions, my clients and I revisit and explore these narratives, comparing and sharing our stories together. The importance of narrative in couples therapy lies in its ability to foster empathy, understanding, and connection. By identifying and challenging dominant narratives or negative patterns, couples can rewrite their stories in ways that empower and inspire growth. Drawing from the narrative pillars of externalizing and deconstructing problems and re-authoring our stories, we can work collaboratively to co-create a new narrative—one that reflects the strengths, resilience, and potential for transformation inherent in their relationship journey. Through this process, couples will discover newfound agency and hope, reclaiming ownership of their story and charting a course toward a more fulfilling and authentic connection. *(We will make our own narrative together in the following sections.)*

I've logged thousands of hours working with couples, sitting with them through the highs and lows of their relationships in hopes of fostering meaningful change in their lives. While the outcomes aren't always easy or happy, I've come to understand the profound impact that therapy can have on couples' lives. Sometimes, therapy facilitates a clear and amicable parting of ways, allowing individuals to move forward with clarity and purpose. Other times, it leads to transformative changes within the relationship, bridging years of pain and distance and fostering a deeper, more fulfilling bond. If there's one thing therapy does, it's create movement.

I got married young, and I consider myself fortunate to have found my life partner at a young age. However, I'm well aware that this isn't the reality for everyone. My journey is just one story among many, and I share it to humanize myself and illustrate that I'm no different from you. Whether you met your person young or later in life, whether you're married, in a long-term relationship, or navigating the complexities of singledom, I'm here to offer genuine help based on my knowledge and experience as both a married person and a marriage therapist. My goal is to meet you where you are, with empathy and understanding, and to support you in creating the relationship you desire.

I have devoted my education and practice to the vital aspects of sexuality wellness and intimacy within relationships. In this book, I aim to share practical strategies for enhancing intimacy, reigniting connection, and addressing areas of intimacy that may have been overlooked or underexplored.

Drawing from my specialized training and extensive experience, I'll guide you through exercises and discussions aimed at deepening your understanding of sexual health and satisfaction. Together, we'll explore ways to reconnect with your partner on a physical and emotional level, fostering a sense of closeness and passion that transcends the mundane routines of daily life. Whether you're seeking to rekindle the flame in a long-term relationship or to embark on a journey of sexual exploration and discovery, this book offers the tools, insights, and education you need to create a more fulfilling and vibrant intimate connection with your partner.

This book is here to guide you in your own journey through the intricacies of relationships. From understanding the fundamental pillars of effective communication to navigating the challenges that inevitably arise, each chapter is designed to offer practical insights and strategies tailored to your unique relationship journey. We'll explore the importance of expressing feelings, taking responsibility, offering compromise, and saying sorry as essential tools for resolving conflicts and deepening emotional connection. Through exercises and reflections, you'll uncover the narrative of your relationship, identifying strengths and areas for growth. Together, we'll delve into the nuances of intimacy and desire, exploring ways to cultivate a more fulfilling and passionate connection with your partner. Whether you're seeking to strengthen your bond, reignite the spark, or navigate a challenging phase in your relationship, this book is your companion on the journey towards a healthier, happier partnership.

So, why therapy, or why did you pick up this book?

Therapy can be a safe space for couples to explore and understand their relationship dynamics. Within this environment, couples can openly discuss their thoughts, feelings, and experiences, fostering deeper insight and connection. Through evidence-based strategies tailored to their unique needs, couples gain valuable tools and insights for growth in communication, intimacy, and conflict resolution, empowering them to navigate challenges and strengthen their bond.

In therapy, setting clear and achievable goals is essential for guiding the process and achieving meaningful outcomes. I work with couples to identify mutual objectives, such as improving communication, resolving conflicts more effectively, or enhancing intimacy. By setting specific, measurable, achievable, realistic, and time-oriented goals, called SMART goals, you can track your progress, stay motivated, and take an active role in shaping their relationship's future.

To create SMART goals for your relationship, start by identifying specific areas you'd like to focus on, such as communication, conflict resolution, and intimacy. For example, a specific goal related to communication could be to practice active listening techniques. To ensure your goal is measurable, consider what success would look like. In this case, you might aim to have at least one uninterrupted conversation per week where each partner practices active listening. Next, assess whether your goal is achievable. How can you realistically implement this practice into your routine? If so, move on to relevance—does this goal align with your overall relationship objectives? Finally, make sure your goal is time-bound by setting a deadline for achievement. For instance, commit to achieving this goal within the next month. When you create goals this way, you can effectively target areas for improvement in your relationship and track your progress over time.

SMART GOALS

Specific	
Measurable	
Achievable	
Realistic	
Time-oriented	

Many couples start therapy in hopes of finding direction, I like to provide that in my first sessions with couples. The landscape of our minds is marked by deeply etched patterns and neural pathways. I aim to help clients gently cover the tracks of unhelpful narratives, while also guiding them in carving out new, healthier narratives within their relationships.

Our narrative is powerful. Through journaling or talking to our friends, it's how we internalize and externalize the world that determines how we feel. Our method of digesting and manifesting our reality fundamentally shapes our emotional world. Our mood is dictated by what we tell ourselves. This makes sense, but when we really apply it intentionally, we can make significant changes in our lives and relationships. Therapy offers a unique opportunity for couples to invest in their relationship and prioritize its growth and well-being. By seeking therapy, you demonstrate a commitment to understanding each other better, improving communication, and building a stronger, more fulfilling connection.

René Descartes' famous declaration, "Cogito, ergo sum," or, "I think, therefore I am," hits at the core of narrative therapy. The idea that our thoughts and the stories we tell ourselves profoundly shape our emotions and actions. By reframing our stories, we have the power to alter our reality and identity. Our self-perception and the world around us are constructed by our internal narratives.

Your Narrative

In narrative therapy, you're not just a passive participant in your therapy journey; you're the lead author of your life story. This approach recognizes that you have important insights into your own experiences. It's all about distinguishing you from the problems you face, reinforcing the idea that while challenges are part of your story, they don't define who you are.

Think of your identity as a book that's constantly being written. Narrative therapy helps you understand that your past chapters don't have to dictate the direction of your future. You're encouraged to rewrite your narrative, opening up possibilities for personal transformation and growth.

One of the unique aspects of narrative therapy is its attention to the larger context of your life. It's not just about what's happening internally; it's also about understanding how cultural, social, and political narratives play a role in shaping your experiences. Approaching it this way gives you a broader perspective on the challenges you face, highlighting how external factors influence your personal narrative. Through these narrative metaphors and focusing on moments that stand out in your story of challenges, you and your therapist can work together to identify and strengthen alternative narratives that align with your best self.

Practical applications of narrative therapy often involve you and, at times, your partner engaging in storytelling and re-authoring your stories, using structured methods to make sure everyone's voice is heard. The success of narrative therapy depends on curiosity, collaboration, and an openness to understand and honor your unique story. It's not just about overcoming challenges but about celebrating your agency, your resilience, and your ability to author your own life and relationship story.

Many of us, if not all of us have or will experience trauma at some point. Comparing our trauma to others doesn't make sense because trauma is not the event that happens to us but the way that we perceive it. This is a good thing and gets at the core of narrative therapy. These invisible influences can be traced back to our childhood experiences, like neglect, chaos, or pain. It's how these experiences continue to resonate within us, influencing our daily lives and shaping our responses to the world around us.

Maybe you have wondered why some people have strong trauma responses to certain events and others are able to cope in a way that doesn't feel traumatic. It's not the past that defines us; it's how the past echoes in our present, in the way we flinch at certain words or the way a particular shade of the evening sky makes us feel.

```
"What matters in life is not what happens to
you but what you remember and how you
remember it."

        -Nobel Prize winner Gabriel García Márquez
```

```
How would you tell your story?
```

Your Table of Contents: Your Stories

I usually give my clients an activity to do on one of their first sessions with me. This exercise is what I call the Table of Contents. It's an exercise where I have each person independently make their own timeline of how they would explain their narrative of the relationship. Often, couples are on different pages about events early on in the relationship or remember certain times of the relationship differently than their partner.

This is an example of how each partner's could look:

> *Chapter 1: the Fall — (meeting, drinking coco @ Jo's, our first fight)
> *Chapter 2: the Spring — (going to Canada, jealousy argument, Tim's Birthday disaster :-))
> *Chapter 3: the Summer — (moved in together, promotion, new puppy)
> *Chapter 4: the Winter — (fighting, Colorado trip, the sorta breakup)

> CHAPTER 1: MEETING & FALLING IN LOVE, THE CAMPING TRIP
>
> CHAPTER 2: GROWING CLOSER, ROCKY ROADS, MY SURPRISE BDAY PARTY
>
> CHAPTER 3: MOVING IN & ADOPTING PUPPY, BIG PROMOTION!

Your narrative as a couple and each of your individual narratives within the relationship hold immense importance in therapy and overall in your dynamics. These narratives serve as the lenses through which you perceive, interpret, and make sense of your shared experiences. In order to foster empathy, communication, and connection within the relationship, you have to understand and explore these narratives.

Firstly, your narrative reflects the collective story of your whole relationship journey. It encompasses the shared experiences, milestones, challenges, and triumphs that have shaped your bond over time. When you examine your narrative together, you gain insight into each other's perspectives, values, and emotional landscapes. This process requires empathy and understanding, laying the foundation for effective communication and mutual support.

On the other hand, each of your narratives offers a unique window into your inner world and personal history. It reveals the stories you tell yourself about your identity, relationships, and life experiences. When you explore these individual narratives, it allows you both to uncover underlying beliefs, fears, and desires that may influence your behavior and interactions within the relationship. By understanding and validating each other's narratives, you can cultivate a deeper sense of intimacy,

Recognizing the differences and intersections between your narratives is crucial for navigating conflicts and fostering resilience. You may discover discrepancies or conflicting interpretations of past events, which can lead to misunderstandings and tension.

Couples often encounter differing interpretations of past events, leading to misunderstandings and tension. These variations arise as partners construct their realities, influenced by unique perspectives and experiences. Memory recall differences and personal biases contribute to conflicting narratives. Therapy offers a space to explore these discrepancies, validate each other's perspectives, and collaboratively reevaluate their shared narrative. By engaging in open dialogue and collaborative exploration, you can bridge these gaps, reconcile differences, and co-create a more cohesive and harmonious narrative of their relationship.

Overall, the narratives are integral components of the therapeutic process. By honoring and exploring these narratives with curiosity, compassion, and openness, you can deepen your connection, strengthen your bond, and build a foundation for lasting love and mutual growth.

Prompt for Reflection

After creating your own timeline, compare and discuss them to gain insight into each other's perspectives, memories, and interpretations of shared experiences.

You can create your own Table of Contents in this book if you like.

Now is your chance to make your own individual Table of Contents.

For this exercise, each of you will independently create a timeline of your relationship, organizing significant events, milestones, and experiences into chapter titles like a book's table of contents. You can give each chapter a creative name or even a subheading. These chapters typically reflect key periods or themes in the relationship journey, such as the beginning stages, major transitions, challenges, and moments of growth or transformation.

Table of Contents

Here are some reflection questions to help you get started, and some to consider after your discussion:

Before Sharing Table of Contents:
- Consider your own narrative of the relationship. Are there any events or experiences you feel hesitant or uncomfortable discussing with your partner? Why?
- What are your expectations or hopes for how your partner will perceive your relationship narrative?
- How do you anticipate your partner's narrative may differ from your own? What aspects of their perspective are you curious or anxious to explore?

After Comparing and Discussing Table of Contents:
- How did sharing and comparing your relationship narratives impact your understanding of each other's perspectives?
- Reflect on any surprises or insights that emerged during the discussion. Did you uncover any new information or perspectives about your relationship?
- Consider any areas of alignment or discrepancy between your narratives. How do you plan to navigate these differences moving forward?
- What emotions arose during the discussion, and how did they influence your connection with your partner? How can you use this newfound understanding to strengthen your relationship?

Emotional Connection & Communication

This chapter is all about improving communication and mutual understanding to help you develop a deeper connection with your partner. You'll discover the basics of communication and how to express your affection in ways that feel emotionally safe. You will learn about attachment types and how your relationship is shaped by past experiences and trauma. With practical tools like quizzes and conflict-resolution phrases, you can improve intimacy and challenge negative beliefs. It's about taking action and making the necessary changes to create a happy relationship primed for intimacy.

Emotional connection helps dictate what your perception of sexual cues and how you are experiencing intimacy as a whole (Herzog, 2024). When you don't feel supported and cannot communicate what you need, your sexual experiences or your desire to have sexual experiences are going to be negatively affected. It is important in addressing the challenges you and your partner are facing with your emotional connection first before addressing your intimate love life.

How can we deepen your understanding and communication with each other?

Love Languages

The well known love languages, coined by Dr. Gary Chapman, Ph.D., offer a unique way to understand and deepen your emotional connection and intimacy within your relationship. To foster healthy bonds, we have to understand how transformative to your relationship it can be to master understanding the language our partner uses.

Richard Warren beautifully encapsulated the essence of love languages when he said, "The most desired gift of love is not diamonds or roses or chocolate. It is focused attention" (Warren, p.83). Uncovering and sharing our love languages is like unlocking a treasure chest of emotional richness, giving us new avenues to express and receive love.

Just as languages have dialects, each person speaks their own unique love language. Through exploration, we'll navigate the five most common love languages:

- Words of Affirmation
- Acts of Service
- Receiving Gifts
- Quality Time
- Physical Touch

Gary Chapman, the creator of the love languages concept, was a Baptist Pastor and not a therapist. Although he had no formal education in therapy, his work brought valuable insights into how we express and receive love. Chapman struggled to provide research or empirical validation for his claims, and instead his extensive experience as a marriage counselor in his church provided many anecdotal examples. It is also important to note that Chapman's views may not fully align with everyone or address their specific needs, particularly within the Neurodivergent/ LGBTQIA+ and Queer/ Consensual/ Ethical Non-Monogamy (CNM/ENM)/ Poly communities, who often find that his "languages" do not address their specific needs or tendencies.

For instance, concepts like info-dumping—where an individual shares a large amount of information on a subject all at once, often seen in neurodivergent communication styles—and pebbling—a more gradual sharing of information and feelings over time—aren't covered but are relevant in these contexts. Despite this, his framework has initiated important conversations about love and relationships.

Exploring love languages isn't just about identifying preferences; it's about empowering you to tailor expressions of affection that deeply resonate with your partner, strengthening your bond and enhancing mutual understanding.

Often, we might default to showing love in the way we like to receive it. For example, if you're all about thoughtful presents, you might find yourself surprising your partner with little gifts, not always remembering that their vibe might be more quality time or words of affirmation.

Recognizing and embracing your partner's love language isn't just romantic—it's strategic. Moments of connection are created when your actions are intentional. Maybe you are all about words, and you're penning love notes or whispering sweet nothings. But, If they appreciate acts of service, your actions might have more of an impact on them. You would want to communicate to them how much you appreciate their words and how you find yourself showing them love this way. We all have our unique ways of feeling loved, and knowing ourselves and our partner allows us to have a common language of understanding. It is important to note that we build emotional intimacy through vulnerability so don't be afraid to mess up or even test out some of the languages to find one that best suits you!

Love Language Quiz

Recognize that sometimes, we may inadvertently express love in the way we wish to receive it. For example, I love picking up tiny trinkets for my husband in the hopes that he will pick up items along his day and give them to me, not remembering that he has their own language preferences.

It's important to not only understand our own love languages but also actively communicate and learn about our partner's preferences. When we do so, we can ensure that our expressions of love are received and appreciated in the most meaningful way possible, deepening our connection and gaining mutual understanding.

Prompt for Reflection

Take a moment to identify your primary love language among the five: Words of Affirmation, Acts of Service, Receiving Gifts, Quality Time, or Physical Touch.

Reflect on specific actions or words that truly make you feel loved and appreciated within your relationship. Consider how you can effectively communicate your love language to your partner, fostering a deeper and more meaningful connection.

Love Language Quiz

Instructions
- For each statement, rate how much you agree on a scale from 1 (not at all) to 5 (Absolutely)
- Add up your scores for each category. The category with the highest total reflects your primary love language.

Words of Affirmation
- I feel loved when my partner tells me how much I mean to them.
- Compliments from my partner make me feel confident and valued.
- Hearing "I love you" is important to me.

Receiving Gifts
- A thoughtful gift from my partner makes me feel special.
- I cherish the gifts my partner gives me because it shows they were thinking of me.
- Surprises and small gifts from my partner brighten my day significantly.

Acts of Service
- I feel cared for when my partner does things to help me out.
- It means a lot to me when my partner goes out of their way to make my life easier.
- Small acts of service from my partner make me feel appreciated.

Quality Time
- I feel most connected to my partner during uninterrupted time spent together.
- Sharing activities or hobbies with my partner is fulfilling for me.
- I appreciate when my partner gives me their full attention, without distractions.

Physical Touch
- A hug or kiss from my partner can instantly lift my mood.
- I feel a strong sense of security and love when my partner holds my hand or touches me.
- Physical closeness with my partner is something I cannot do without.

Emotional Safety

In every relationship, creating emotional safety is paramount to fostering trust, understanding, and intimacy. Our brains, particularly the portion of the brain called the amygdala, play a crucial role in this process. When faced with perceived threats, the amygdala triggers fear responses commonly known as fight, flight, freeze, or fawn. Many are not familiar with the fawn response of appeasement and excessive people-pleasing to avoid conflict and ensure safety. All of these responses are automatic, and they manifest when our anxiety spikes or we become agitated or angry.

In moments of heightened emotion, it's essential to recognize these fear responses in ourselves and our partners. Understanding that these reactions stem from a primal instinct to protect ourselves can help remind ourselves of empathy and compassion in our interactions. When we acknowledge and validate each other's feelings, we can create that safe space where vulnerability is embraced rather than feared.

It's crucial to have an open conversation about your fears, triggers, and past experiences of feeling unsafe with your partner. If you share your vulnerabilities it fosters understanding and allows you to support each other better. It enables you to identify potential triggers and establish boundaries to ensure your emotional safety within the relationship.

Nurturing emotional safety requires patience, empathy, and open communication. Recognizing and addressing how you both respond to fear is important to cultivating a relationship environment where you both feel valued, heard, and secure in expressing your true selves.

Prompt for Reflection:

Take a moment to recall a time when either you or your partner felt unsafe expressing emotions within your relationship.

- How did this affect your communication and connection?

Now, consider the emotional safety practices you can establish to ensure both of you always feel secure in sharing your deepest thoughts and feelings.

- When was a moment when vulnerability felt daunting?

Think of practices to ensure such moments are met with understanding, creating safety and trust.

Attachment & Intimacy

Understanding our style of attachment and connection to our partner(s) helps us understand how our emotions determine our emotional safety during intimacy, or how comfortable we feel engaging with others in an intimate way. Similar to the love languages discussed previously, attachment styles are the unique behaviors, words, and feelings we utilize to engage in intimacy with ourselves and others. These attachment styles are largely influenced by childhood experiences, and what can seem like trivial or inconsequential childhood experiences in memory, can actually manifest themselves as physical, mental, or emotional roadblocks of consequential sizes in our journey of intimacy.

Conceptualizing and deeply grasping this intertwined connection between attachment styles and intimacy through personal settings such as introspection, meditation, and therapy can be the difference between an intimate experience where you feel detached and an intimate experience where you feel present, engaged, and satisfied.

For example, if a strong bond existed between you and your guardian(s) when you were growing up, it can be much easier for you to become comfortable, close, and secure with your partner(s); this can mean many things from less hesitance to share about yourself, less resistance to expressing vulnerability, and more comfortability in intimacy. If someone did not have a stable, strong bond with their guardians, the inverse can be true; emotions can be hard to discuss and share, walling themselves up is much easier than being vulnerable, and the deep-rooted trust desired for connected intimacy can feel unattainable.

According to the diathesis-stress model, individuals who were exposed to stressful life circumstances stemming from shaky bonds with their guardians in their youth are more likely to develop anxiety disorders, one of the leading causes of dissatisfaction and intimacy challenges in adulthood.

Our biology and genetic makeup are wired in our brains from birth and plays a big role in this. For example, if a mother is overly sensitive or anxious it could lead her child to develop standoffish or avoidant tendencies when it comes to forming close bonds later in her child's life, and if there are big disruptions or long periods of emotional instability during childhood, it can make these tendencies even stronger.

ATTACHMENT STYLES

ANXIOUS ATTACHMENT
- High need for approval and reassurance
- Fear of abandonment and rejection
- Intense emotional highs and lows
- Tendency to be overly dependent on relationships

DISMISSIVE-AVOIDANT ATTACHMENT
- Discomfort with closeness & emotional expression
- Emphasis on independence and self-sufficiency
- Tendency to suppress emotions & avoid dependency
- May appear aloof or emotionally-distant

FEARFUL-AVOIDANT ATTACHMENT
- Inconsistent & contradictory behaviors
- Desire for closeness combined with fear of intimacy
- Difficulty regulating emotions and forming stable relationships
- Often associated with trauma or unresolved issues from childhood

SECURE ATTACHMENT
- Comfortable with closeness and autonomy
- Positive view of self and others
- Ability to form stable and trusting relationships
- Effective communication and emotion regulation

All this ties back to the importance of knowing how your own mind ticks, especially when dealing with stress or anxiety. It's more about understanding how you're feeling in the here and now, instead of getting stuck on what happened in the past.

Anxiously attached individuals seeking emotional closeness and connection may often find themselves paired with partners exhibiting avoidant attachment tendencies. If you're someone who seeks deep emotional closeness, you might end up with partners who aren't as comfortable with intimacy. These individuals sometimes have an inherent temperament that leads to automatic dysregulation in emotionally charged or vulnerable situations.

If you're showing signs of an **anxious avoidant attachment**, you might find yourself pushing back against your partner's emotional moments, maybe even asking, "Why are you making such a big deal out of this?" or saying, "Chill out, it's not that serious." You could also brush off serious relationship talks like they're nothing, throwing out "It's not a big deal to me" or "Whatever, I don't care." or "get off my back". This dynamic can really throw a wrench in getting close to each other.

If you have an **anxious-avoidant attachment style**, you might find yourself dodging the "What are we?" convo or shying away from real talks about how things are going between you and your partner. You could brush off their worries, keep your own gripes under wraps, and get all defensive when deep relationship conversations come up. This might look like you making up excuses, playing down your partner's concerns, or getting super annoyed if they keep pressing for a heart-to-heart. It's like putting up walls instead of opening up, which can make navigating through relationship issues way harder.

Keeping emotional intimacy at arm's length is a common trait for those with an **avoidant attachment style**. This behavior often traces back to childhood experiences like feeling neglected, abandoned, or rejected. It's not just about past experiences, though; some folks are just wired to automatically pull back when things get too emotionally intense. This can make deep connections and open communication tough in relationships. They might brush off their partner's feelings, avoid deep talks, or dodge putting a label on the relationship. When issues pop up, instead of facing them head-on, they might shut down or sidestep the conversation, making it challenging to bridge the emotional gap.

Understanding attachment and intimacy dynamics is pivotal in navigating the complexities of relationships. Whether it's anxious-avoidant attachment patterns or avoidant tendencies, recognizing these behaviors sheds light on how past experiences and innate temperament influence present-day interactions. By fostering awareness and empathy towards oneself and others, individuals can cultivate healthier attachment styles, fostering deeper emotional connections and more fulfilling relationships.

Core Negative Beliefs Challenged in Arguments

Our minds create powerful narratives that shape our reality, especially when dealing with fears and doubts. These narratives, often rooted in core negative beliefs, can deeply influence our perceptions and interactions.

Dr. Angelica Shiels (2024) explains that intrusive thoughts can occur in everyone. For example, you might suddenly worry about something distressing or unlikely happening, especially when feeling powerless or afraid. The problem isn't the intrusive thoughts themselves but the meaning we attach to them. Individuals with clinical anxiety often believe that their thoughts define their reality, leading to insecurity and self-doubt.

People might internalize stigma, believing negative thoughts about their identity are true reflections of themselves. This "magical thinking" makes them believe their thoughts inherently define reality. Dr. Shiels points out that many postpartum women have fleeting thoughts of harming their infants. Those who believe these thoughts mean something significant are more likely to develop postpartum depression and anxiety. This illustrates that it's not the intrusive thoughts themselves but the meaning we attach to them that causes distress.

In relationships, especially during arguments, our core beliefs are often challenged, triggering fear and activating our attachment styles. When we feel threatened, our deeply held beliefs about ourselves can flare up, leading to defensive or anxious behavior. Recognizing and understanding these core beliefs can help us navigate conflicts more effectively and foster healthier communication with our partners.

The following section includes a comprehensive list of 126 negative core beliefs that can impact our relationships. These beliefs are detailed over the next several pages, offering insights into how they manifest and affect your life. By reading through these core beliefs and identifying the ones that resonate with you, you can gain a deeper understanding of your internal narratives. This self-awareness can be a powerful tool in resolving conflicts and improving your relationships.

```
You can take some time to look at the next
section by yourself or with your partner.

Note: some core beliefs will be repeated
```

Attachment Styles and Related Beliefs

Secure Attachment

You generally feel confident in your relationship, but occasionally worry about not being heard or valued by your partner. For instance, when you express your feelings about household chores like doing the dishes, and your partner doesn't seem to listen, you might feel temporarily inadequate or unimportant, but these feelings usually pass quickly, allowing you to maintain a healthy connection with your partner.

1. I am unimportant.
2. I am not capable.

Anxious Attachment

In your relationship, you often feel anxious and fear that your partner will leave you. When your partner doesn't reply to your messages quickly, you constantly seek reassurance and struggle with feelings of being unlovable and not good enough, which can lead to clinginess and emotional distress, causing tension in your relationship.

3. I am not good enough.
4. I am unworthy.
5. I am unlovable.
6. I am too much.
7. I am a burden.

Attachment Styles and Related Beliefs in Relationships (continued)

Avoidant Attachment

You prefer to keep a safe distance in your relationship, fearing that too much closeness will lead to a loss of independence. When your partner wants to discuss future plans or have deep conversations, you often believe you are better off alone and are wary of becoming too vulnerable or dependent on your partner, which can create emotional distance between you and your partner.

8. I am better off alone.

9. I am unworthy of love.

10. I am vulnerable.

11. I am unfit for relationships.

12. I am out of control.

Fearful-Avoidant Attachment (Disorganized)

You experience a push-pull dynamic in your relationship, desiring intimacy but fearing it at the same time. When your partner tries to get close or build trust after a previous betrayal, you often feel unsafe and powerless, leading to erratic behavior and deep-seated trust issues, making it challenging to maintain a stable and secure relationship.

13. I am unworthy.

14. I am unsafe.

15. I am powerless.

16. I am not enough.

17. I am destined to be hurt.

Fears and Beliefs in Relationships

Not Being Listened To

You feel invisible in your relationship and worry that your thoughts and feelings don't matter to your partner. For instance, when you talk about needing more support around the house, like the dishes, and your partner doesn't respond, you often doubt your worthiness of attention and can become withdrawn or overly accommodating to avoid conflict, which can lead to feelings of frustration and isolation.

18. I am invisible.

19. I am unimportant.

20. I am not worth attention.

Not Being Respected

You struggle with self-worth and frequently feel disrespected by your partner. When your partner dismisses your opinions during discussions, you believe you are not good enough and fear that your opinions and needs are undervalued, leading to frustration and resentment, which can create tension and conflict in your relationship.

21. I am not worth respect.

22. I am not good enough.

23. I am flawed.

Fears of Not Being Treated as Equal

You often feel inferior in your relationship, fearing you are not capable or worthy of equality. When decisions are made without your input, you believe you are unworthy of equality, causing you to accept unequal roles and contributions, leading to a sense of imbalance and dissatisfaction, which can affect the overall health and stability of your relationship.

24. I am inferior.

25. I am not capable.

26. I am unworthy of equality.

Core Negative Beliefs in Relationships

Self-Worth

You constantly feel like a failure and struggle with self-esteem issues. When you can't seem to get a promotion at work, you believe you are unworthy of success and happiness, which impacts your confidence and can create distance between you and your partner as you doubt your own value in the relationship.

27. I am not good enough.
28. I am unworthy.
29. I am a failure.
30. I am unimportant.
32. I am unlovable.
31. I am insignificant.
32. I am unlovable.
33. I am a disappointment.
34. I am undeserving of success.
35. I am undeserving of happiness.
36. I am unworthy of respect.

Core Negative Beliefs in Relationships (continued)

Identity and Self-Concept

You feel fundamentally flawed and defective, often believing you are broken beyond repair. When your partner points out a mistake you made, these negative self-concepts lead you to isolate yourself and avoid forming close relationships, which can make it difficult for your partner to connect with you on a deeper level.

37. I am flawed.
38. I am defective.
39. I am broken.
40. I am weak.
41. I am stupid.
42. I am inferior.
43. I am untrustworthy.
44. I am unlovable.
45. I am ugly.
46. I am dirty.

Core Negative Beliefs in Relationships (continued)

Belonging & Connection

You feel a profound sense of loneliness and believe you don't belong anywhere. When you see your partner enjoying social events without you, you often think you are unfit for relationships and destined to be alone, which hinders your ability to connect with your partner and can create feelings of isolation and disconnection.

47. I am alone.
48. I don't belong.
49. I am unwanted.
50. I am unfit for relationships.
51. I am destined to be alone.
52. I am unworthy of being seen.
53. I am too different.
54. I am destined to be hurt.
55. I am invisible.
56. I am a burden.

Core Negative Beliefs in Relationships (continued)

Safety & Security

You feel constantly unsafe and powerless, fearing that something bad will happen at any moment. When your partner is late coming home and doesn't call, this belief leads to hypervigilance and difficulty trusting others, impacting your relationship and overall well-being as you struggle to feel secure and supported.

57. I am unsafe.

58. I am powerless.

59. I am helpless.

60. I am out of control.

61. I am unworthy of protection.

62. I am not capable.

63. I am vulnerable.

64. I am weak.

65. I am unworthy of safety.

66. I am destined to be harmed.

Core Negative Beliefs in Relationships (continued)

Responsibility & Guilt

You feel responsible for everyone else's happiness and blame yourself for any problems that arise. When there's tension in your relationship, you struggle with guilt and shame, believing you are a bad person who is always at fault, which can lead to self-sacrifice and resentment in your relationship as you take on more than your share of responsibility.

67. I am responsible for others' happiness.
68. I am responsible for everything.
69. I am unworthy of forgiveness.
70. I am to blame.
71. I am a mistake.
72. I am shameful.
73. I am guilty.
74. I am wrong.
75. I am a bad person.
76. I am a problem.

Core Negative Beliefs in Relationships (continued)

Competence & Achievement

You doubt your abilities and believe you are incompetent and destined to fail. When you struggle to complete a project at work, this lack of confidence affects your career and personal ambitions, leading to a reluctance to take risks or pursue your goals, which can create tension in your relationship as your partner may struggle to understand your hesitancy.

77. I am not enough.
78. I am not capable.
79. I am incompetent.
80. I am destined to fail.
81. I am unable to change.
82. I am not intelligent.
83. I am unworthy of success.
84. I am not creative.
85. I am not skilled.
86. I am not talented.

Core Negative Beliefs in Relationships (continued)

Control and Autonomy

You feel out of control in your life and believe you are incapable of making decisions. When you rely heavily on your partner to make plans or decisions, fearing that you cannot take care of yourself or be self-sufficient, this can create a dynamic of dependency and imbalance in your relationship.

87. I am out of control.

88. I am powerless.

89. I am weak-willed.

90. I am dependent.

91. I am incapable of making decisions.

92. I am unable to take care of myself.

93. I am not autonomous.

94. I am not self-sufficient.

95. I am a follower.

96. I am easily controlled.

Core Negative Beliefs in Relationships (continued)

Emotional Expression

You feel that your emotions are too intense and fear expressing them will push your partner away. When you suppress your feelings about your partner's behavior, believing you are too sensitive and dramatic, this leads to internal emotional conflict, creating distance and misunderstandings in your relationship.

97. I am too much.

98. I am too emotional.

99. I am too sensitive.

100. I am too needy.

101. I am too intense.

102. I am too demanding.

103. I am too dramatic.

104. I am not allowed to express my feelings.

105. I am not allowed to be angry.

106. I am not allowed to cry.

Core Negative Beliefs in Relationships (continued)

Relationships and Social Interactions

You feel you are unlovable and unwanted, fearing rejection in every relationship. When your partner interacts warmly with others but seems distant with you, you believe you are not good at social interactions and are always judged, which causes you to avoid social situations and intimacy, impacting your ability to build and maintain close relationships.

107. I am unlovable.

108. I am unwanted.

109. I am always judged.

110. I am not worthy of love.

111. I am not worthy of friendship.

113. I am destined to be rejected.

113. I am not good at relationships.

114. I am not socially adept.

115. I am always misunderstood.

Core Negative Beliefs in Relationships (continued)

Physical Self

You feel unattractive and are highly critical of your physical appearance. When your partner doesn't compliment you or seem attracted to you, you believe you are ugly and unhealthy, which impacts your self-esteem and confidence in forming romantic relationships, leading to insecurities and challenges in connecting with your partner.

117. I am ugly.
118. I am unattractive.
119. I am fat.
120. I am too skinny.
121. I am too short.
122. I am too tall.
123. I am unhealthy.
124. I am physically weak.
125. I am not athletic.
126. I am not beautiful.

Apology & Repair

After reading the negative core beliefs, if any have resonated with you, make note of them and talk about them together. When we don't repair conflicts, especially intense ones, it can strain our relationships. Effective de-escalation techniques like deep breathing, active listening, time-outs, and conflict analysis are helpful and can reduce emotional distress and foster constructive communication. Obviously this can help deescalate a situation but engaging in these practices isn't just about cooling off; it's about transforming a potentially explosive situation into an opportunity for growth and understanding. Sincere apologies are incredibly important to the delicate process of repairing relationships post-conflict. As we now know, repair is the most important part of any conflict mending. In this section we will discuss how to strategically communicate and work on reassuring these feelings.

Methods of apology and repair are their own languages; when it comes to saying "sorry", everyone has their own unique dialect with their words and/or actions. Understanding your partner's apology and repair method, as well as your own, can save you emotional distress by being able to translate what they are trying to say, even if you speak a different tongue.

Down the path of apologetic vocalization, some people are direct, cutting straight to the heart of the matter with a simple "I was wrong, and I'm sorry." This language is easy to speak and understand as it offers little wiggle room to misinterpret the apology someone is attempting to convey. On the emotional front, some pour out their guilt and regret in a wave of sincerity that leaves no doubt of their remorse. Conversely, some people prefer to choose subtle, indirect ways to express remorse like lightening the mood with a joke or offering indirect gestures of apology.

Some individuals prefer the explanatory route, sharing the *why* behind the mistake in the hopes of painting a clearer picture of their intentions that unfortunately went awry. It is important to realize that an explanation does not always equate to a defensive posture, or someone digging their heels in making sure they stand their ground in an attempt to not apologize, but rather it can truly represent someone realizing they hurt you or made a mistake, and are attempting to explain why or how they made the mistake in the first place.

Then there are those who believe actions speak volumes, where a hug or act of service serves as their way of making amends. Some individuals may take a physically reparative approach such as cleaning up around the house or tackling a chore or errand that their partner was planning on doing.

Finally, there are those seriously committed to change, who not only directly, vocally apologize but also set in motion specific actions to ensure history doesn't repeat itself. I personally am sensitive and prefer a gentle, sincere, meaningful apology followed by amends. Sometimes, I also appreciate my partner reminding me that we are on the same team by saying, "Same Team," which reminds me to feel secure in the relationship when I am upset.

Come up with codewords and phrases to use when you want to make sure that everything is repaired. They can be silly!

Understanding and recognizing all the diverse apology languages can lead to deeper empathy and a stronger connection. At the end of the day, we're all just trying our best to navigate the complexities of human relationships and conflicts within them.

Strategies for Genuine Apologies and Relationship Repair:

- Understand their apology language. Different individuals resonate with different distinct forms of apologies, making it crucial to tailor apologies to your partner for them to be meaningful.

- You have to take responsibility, genuinely accept responsibility, and communicate remorse.

- Make amends, as it is the action of an apology. Understand the significance of proactive steps in rectifying harm and rebuilding trust.

- Repairing is paramount. Use emotional language and the "Essential Phrases for Mending Conflict" (found below) to build trust through open communication.

- After looking at the phrases, discuss with your partner which phrases work and which ones will cause more tension.

Apology Languages

While apology languages provide a structured framework for understanding how individuals prefer to give and receive apologies, apology styles offer insight into the broader patterns and manners in which apologies are expressed.

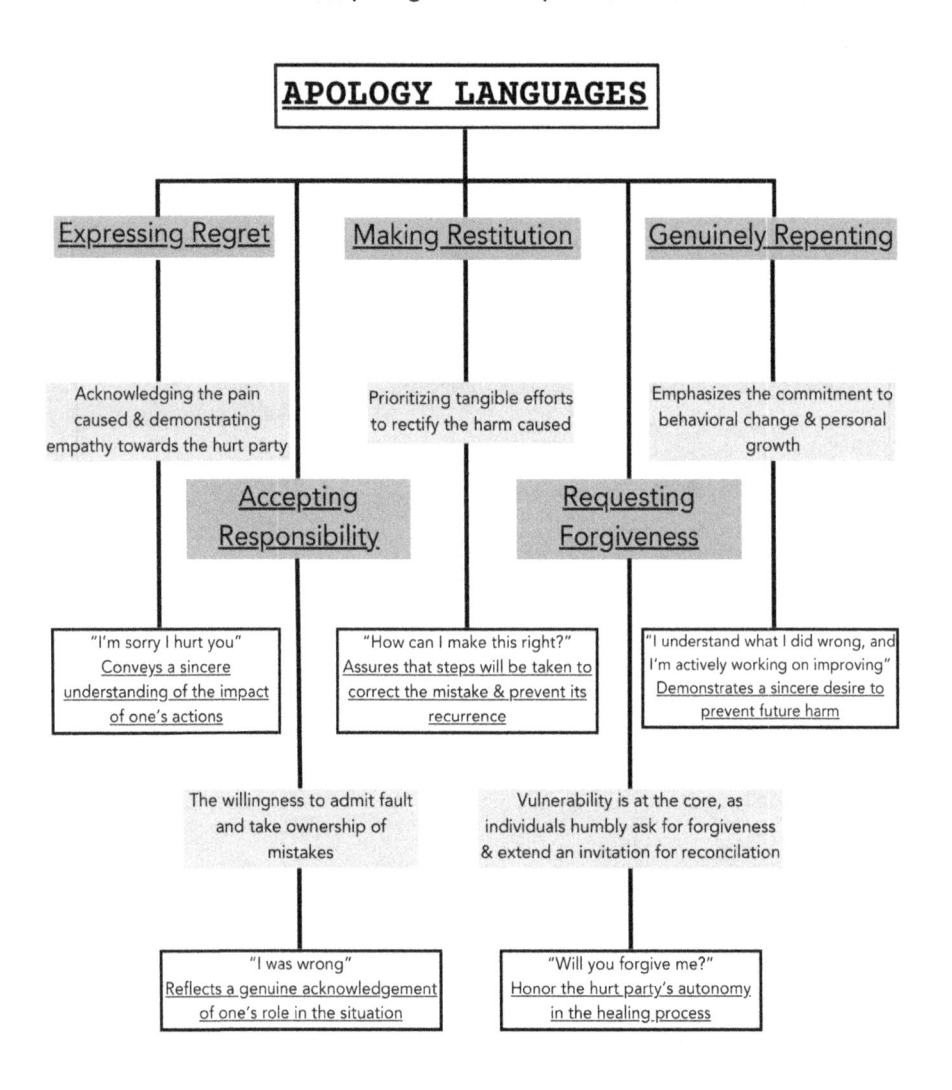

APOLOGY LANGUAGES

Expressing Regret
Acknowledging the pain caused & demonstrating empathy towards the hurt party

"I'm sorry I hurt you"
Conveys a sincere understanding of the impact of one's actions

Making Restitution
Prioritizing tangible efforts to rectify the harm caused

"How can I make this right?"
Assures that steps will be taken to correct the mistake & prevent its recurrence

Genuinely Repenting
Emphasizes the commitment to behavioral change & personal growth

"I understand what I did wrong, and I'm actively working on improving"
Demonstrates a sincere desire to prevent future harm

Accepting Responsibility
The willingness to admit fault and take ownership of mistakes

"I was wrong"
Reflects a genuine acknowledgement of one's role in the situation

Requesting Forgiveness
Vulnerability is at the core, as individuals humbly ask for forgiveness & extend an invitation for reconciliation

"Will you forgive me?"
Honor the hurt party's autonomy in the healing process

APOLOGY STYLES

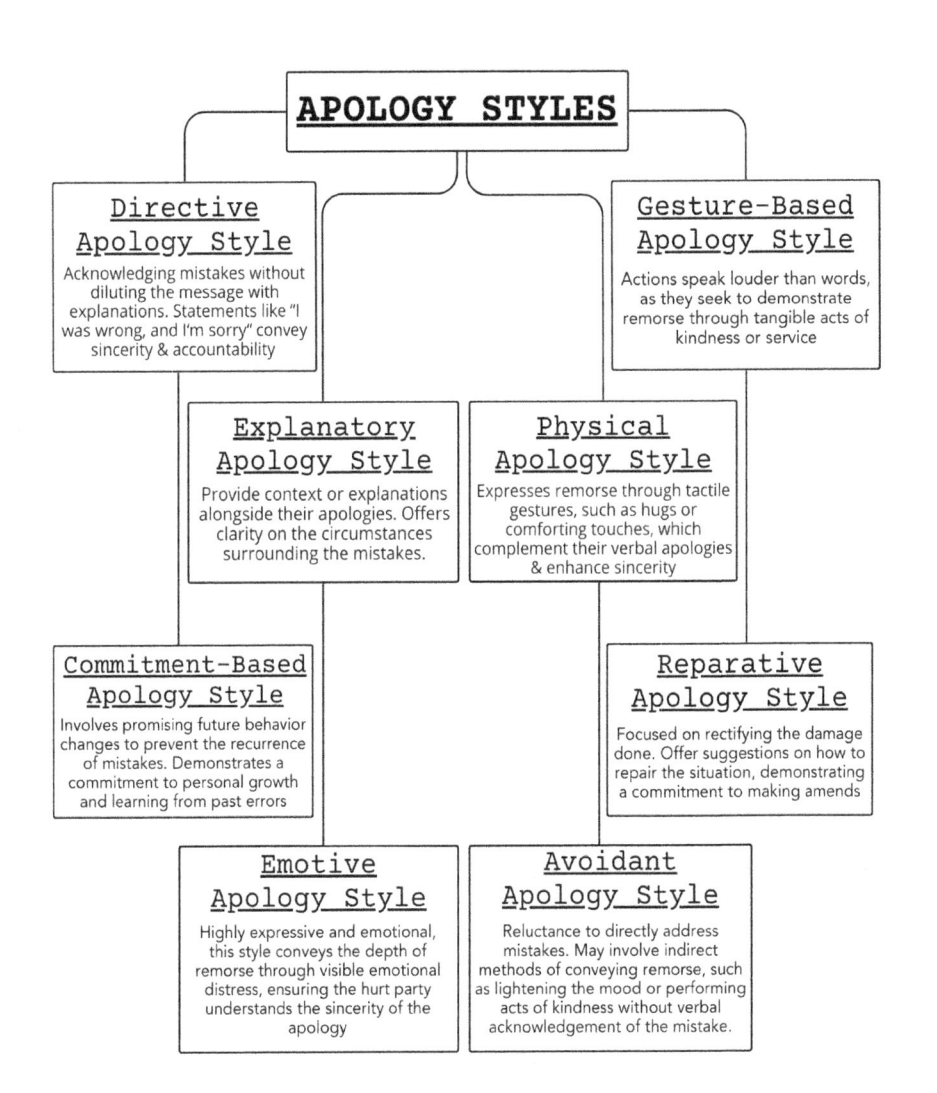

Directive Apology Style
Acknowledging mistakes without diluting the message with explanations. Statements like "I was wrong, and I'm sorry" convey sincerity & accountability

Gesture-Based Apology Style
Actions speak louder than words, as they seek to demonstrate remorse through tangible acts of kindness or service

Explanatory Apology Style
Provide context or explanations alongside their apologies. Offers clarity on the circumstances surrounding the mistakes.

Physical Apology Style
Expresses remorse through tactile gestures, such as hugs or comforting touches, which complement their verbal apologies & enhance sincerity

Commitment-Based Apology Style
Involves promising future behavior changes to prevent the recurrence of mistakes. Demonstrates a commitment to personal growth and learning from past errors

Reparative Apology Style
Focused on rectifying the damage done. Offer suggestions on how to repair the situation, demonstrating a commitment to making amends

Emotive Apology Style
Highly expressive and emotional, this style conveys the depth of remorse through visible emotional distress, ensuring the hurt party understands the sincerity of the apology

Avoidant Apology Style
Reluctance to directly address mistakes. May involve indirect methods of conveying remorse, such as lightening the mood or performing acts of kindness without verbal acknowledgement of the mistake.

Tip: Using "I feel..." statements can help give you a simple framework to start your apologies.

Prompt for Reflection

Consider a time when you had to offer or receive an apology in your relationship. Describe the experience and its impact on trust and understanding. If you could redo the apology or repair process, what would you do differently?

Reflecting on the apology languages and styles discussed, consider a time when you received an apology that resonated with you deeply, even if it was delivered in a style different from your preferred one. How did this experience impact your perception of the apology and the person offering it?

How can understanding and acknowledging the various apology languages and styles enhance your ability to navigate conflicts and foster reconciliation in your relationships?

Essential Phrases for Mending Conflict:

EXPRESSIVE FEELINGS

- I feel uneasy about what just happened.
- I need a moment to express my thoughts carefully.
- I'm experiencing a strong reaction, and I want to understand why.
- It's difficult for me to say this, but I feel hurt.
- I'm feeling overwhelmed and need to share my feelings.
- I feel anxious and need to talk about it.
- I'm feeling disconnected and want to bridge that gap.
- My emotions are complex right now; I need to unpack them with you.
- I'm feeling neglected and want to address this feeling.

TAKING RESPONSIBILITY

- I recognized my part in this situation.
- I might have missed the mark on that one.
- It's clear to me now how my actions affected you.
- I want to be accountable for what I've said and done.
- I understand that my behavior had consequences.
- I see now how I could have approached that differently.
- I should have been more sensitive to your feelings.
- I neglected to consider your perspective, and I regret that.
- I owe you an apology for jumping to conclusions.

EXPRESSING GRATITUDE

- I appreciate your patience with me.
- You're perspective is valuable, and I'm grateful for it.
- Thank you for listening; it means a lot to me.
- I'm thankful for the effort that you're putting into this conversation.
- It's important for me to acknowledge the good in what you're doing.
- I'm grateful for your understanding and empathy.
- Your support means the world to me, especially now.
- I value your willingness to work through this with me.
- It means a lot that you're standing by me through this.

OFFERING COMPROMISE

- Let's find a middle ground on this.
- I am open to blending our ideas together.
- How about we both give a little to reach an agreement?
- Can we meet halfway on this issue?
- I'm willing to adjust my stance if it helps us move forward.
- Let's each suggest a solution and find a middle path.
- What if we each take turns explaining our ideal outcome, then find a blend?
- I think we both have valid points; let's combine them.
- Compromising here could help us both feel more fulfilled.

SAYING SORRY

- I'm sorry for any pain I've caused.
- My apologies for not seeing your side clearly.
- I regret not being more understanding.
- I didn't mean to cause conflict, and I'm sorry.
- I'm sorry for not being attentive to your needs.
- I'm sorry for not considering how my words might affect you.
- I apologize for letting my emotions get the better of me.
- I'm sorry for any misunderstanding I've caused.
- I regret not being there when you needed me.

CONFLICT MANAGEMENT

- Can we pause and come back to this with clear heads?
- Let's try to speak calmly and respectfully to each other.
- It's important for both of us to feel heard and respected.
- Can we discuss this without blaming each other?
- How can we resolve this in a way that works for both of us?
- Let's identify the core issue before it escalates.
- How about we express our feelings without accusations?
- Can we agree to not interrupt each other and listen fully?
- Let's each take a moment to cool down, then resume this conversation.

THIS INFORMATION IS FROM THE FIRST ZINE I MADE, CALLED "MENDING CONFLICT: ESSENTIAL PHRASES FOR MENDING CONFLICT IN RELATIONSHIPS & ATTACHMENT THEORY ZINE 01"

ACE Scores Test

The Adverse Childhood Experiences (ACE) Test was developed by Drs. Vincent Felitti, Robert Anda, and their colleagues as part of a landmark study in 1998 that linked childhood abuse and household dysfunction to many of the leading causes of death in adults.

This study emphasized the significant impact of early adversities on long-term health and behavior, as described in their research titled "Relationship of childhood abuse and household dysfunction to many of the leading causes of death in adults: The Adverse Childhood Experiences (ACE) Study" (Felitti et al., 1998). This test serves as a critical tool for recognizing how such early experiences can profoundly shape one's life.

Trigger Warning: *This test may bring up sensitive or traumatic memories related to past experiences. Please ensure you are in a safe and supportive environment when engaging with this material, and consider using self-soothing techniques or seeking professional support if needed.*

Interpreting Your Score:

- 0-1 Points: Few or no childhood adversities.
- 2-4 Points: Moderate level of childhood adversity.
- 5+ Points: High level of childhood adversity.

Here are the 10 questions that form the core of the ACE test, each question reflects an aspect of childhood adversity identified in the ACE study.

Respond "Yes" if you experienced any of the following before your 18th birthday:

1. Did a parent or other adult in the household often or very often swear at you, insult you, put you down, or humiliate you? Or act in a way that makes you afraid that you might be physically hurt?

2. Did a parent or other adult in the household often or very often push, grab, slap, or throw something at you? Or ever hit you so hard that you had marks or were injured?

3. Did an adult or person at least 5 years older than you ever touch or fondle you or have you touch their body in a sexual way? Or attempt or actually have oral, anal, or vaginal intercourse with you?

4. Did you often or very often feel that no one in your family loved you or thought you were important or special? Or your family didn't feel

close, support, or look out for each other?

5. Did you often or very often feel that you didn't have enough to eat, had to wear dirty clothes, and had no one to protect you? Or your parents were too drunk or high to take care of you or take you to the doctor if you needed it?

6. Were your parents ever separated or divorced?

7. Was your mother or stepmother: Often or very often pushed, grabbed, slapped, or had something thrown at her? Or sometimes, often, or very often kicked, bitten, hit with a fist, or hit with something hard? Or ever repeatedly hit at least a few minutes or threatened with a gun or knife?

8. Did you live with anyone who was a problem drinker or alcoholic, or who used street drugs?

9. Was a household member depressed or mentally ill, or did a household member attempt suicide?

10. Did a household member go to prison?

Our History Informs Our Now

Our childhood experiences have a huge impact on how we handle stress, conflict and relationships. Adverse Childhood Experiences (ACEs) can leave a lasting impact, leading to patterns that persist into adulthood. These early traumas can affect our behavior. How we respond to stress makes it tough to deal with life's obstacles effectively. Research shows that having an ACE score of more than five significantly increases the risk of mental health issues, chronic diseases, difficulties in personal relationships, and issues related to sexual well-being.

One of the most interesting concepts I've come across is "learned helplessness," as discussed by Dr. Emily Nagoski and Dr. Amelia Nagoski. This phenomenon, first identified through a study involving rats, illustrates the impact of uncontrollable stressors on behavior and mental state.

In the study, rats were first exposed to an aversive stimulus, such as an electrical shock. Naturally, the rats tried to escape the stimulus. However, when subjected to an unwinnable task, like a "forced swim test" where they couldn't reach dry land no matter how hard they tried, they eventually gave up and just floated instead of swimming. This surrender extended beyond their enclosure: when returned to an environment with the aversive stimulus, the rats didn't even try to escape. Their experience with the swim tank had taught them that efforts to escape were pointless—a clear manifestation of learned helplessness.

Interestingly, the study found a gender difference in the rats' responses: female rats struggled almost twice as long as male rats in the face of insurmountable odds before giving up.

This concept of learned helplessness isn't confined to just animals; it has huge implications for us as humans, especially when we are often under chronic low-level stressors. Learned helplessness is the belief that your actions have no impact on outcomes, leading to a sense of powerlessness and inaction. For instance, in a relationship, a person might stop trying to improve their behavior despite having access to helpful resources, feeling that their efforts will not make a difference.

Similar experiments with humans have shown that once individuals recognize that a task is rigged or a situation is unwinnable, they begin to feel better. Understanding and acknowledging the nature of chronic stress and how it affects our desire and arousal can significantly alleviate the psychological impact. If you are a woman/AFAB or spend time with women, I highly recommend reading Dr. Nagoskis' work, and especially her book "Come as You Are".

Our Nervous System & Polyvagal Theory

Similar to analyzing ACEs, Polyvagal Theory provides a framework to help us understand how our nervous system reacts to stress and trauma. According to the theory our autonomic nervous system functions in primary three states that you flow in and out of:

> **Ventral Vagal State (Safety and Social Engagement):**
>
> When we feel safe, our ventral vagal system is active, promoting feelings of connection and calm.

> **Sympathetic State (Fight or Flight):**
>
> When we perceive threats the sympathetic system kicks in preparing us for fight or flight responses.

> **Dorsal Vagal State (Shutdown or Freeze):**
>
> When threats seem insurmountable and unavoidable the dorsal vagal system may trigger a shutdown. Freeze reaction, similar to the concept of learned helplessness.

POLYVAGAL THEORY

FLOW BETWEEN STATES EASILY

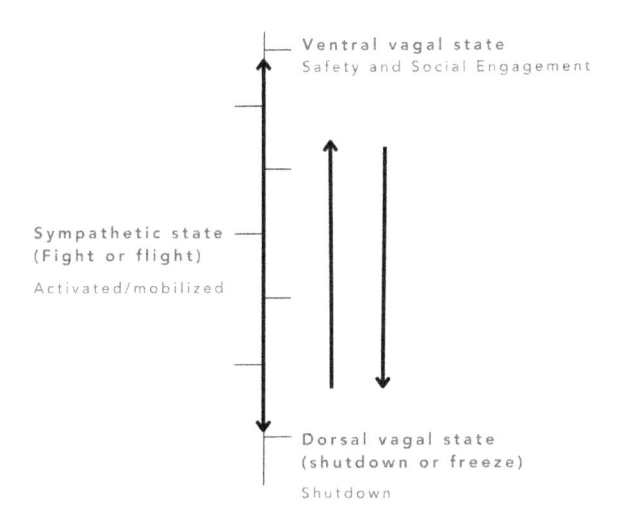

Ventral vagal state
Safety and Social Engagement

Sympathetic state
(Fight or flight)
Activated/mobilized

Dorsal vagal state
(shutdown or freeze)
Shutdown

When we understand these states and when we are in them, we can identify our physiological responses to stress and develop strategies to move towards a state of safety and connection.

Our Adverse Childhood Experiences (ACE) scores provide significant insight into how our past traumas influence our present behavior and stress responses. Higher ACE scores often correlate with greater sensitivity to stress and a higher propensity for learned helplessness. Higher ACE scores can also lead to people being at a higher risk for a plethora of health conditions. When you can understand and communicate about your ACE scores, you can help mend deep-seated roots of stress responses and conflicts. Chronic stress can kill the mood for sex, so it's important to find good ways to relax before getting intimate. Understanding your ACE score is crucial, as it helps identify personal factors that may impact your sexual health.

As we talk more about trauma, this framework can be something to come back to.

Moving into a State of Action

The ideas we've explored provide us with context on how we perceive our sexuality and nervous systems. In partnerships, it's common for couples to encounter chronic stress factors such, as financial concerns, job demands, or unresolved personal issues that may evoke feelings of powerlessness. This becomes particularly evident when conflicts seem insurmountable or persistently resurface resulting in a pattern of tension and acceptance.

In the realm of sexuality, this learned helplessness can manifest as a diminished sexual desire or a feeling of disconnection from your partner. The stress response activated by unresolved conflicts can lead to a state where individuals no longer attempt to address or improve their sexual relationship, believing that change is impossible.

The interplay between sexuality and our nervous system highlights the importance of "set and setting." This phrase is usually used in the context of psychedelics but we are applying it to how we approach sexuality. "Set" refers to the internal mindset, including emotional state and expectations, while "setting" refers to the external environment. Both significantly impact sexual experiences and the ability to engage fully with your partner.

The problem is not stress itself but rather our ineffective strategies we use to address the physiological reactions our bodies have to stressors. It is crucial to adopt active, intentional efforts to manage stress rather than passively accepting it.

Mobilizing into a state of action requires recognizing and addressing the structural forces contributing to how you feel in your body. This means understanding the specific stressors within a relationship and addressing them collectively. Self-care and community care are crucial in this process. When we understand our nervous system and the sources of our stress, we can better tailor strategies, like breathing, grounding ourselves, meditation, or even going for a short walk for relief.

Sex, Pleasure, & Intimacy

This next section covers the essentials of building a strong relationship: creating emotional safety, resolving conflicts, and understanding each other. Creating emotional safety, repairing conflict, and understanding each other are fundamental, but let's be real—sex can be really exciting, and maybe you're just skipping to this part of the book.

We'll talk about why intimacy matters, why sex can get trickier the longer you're together, and how to keep things exciting. From practical tips in sex therapy about desire, difficulties, and the impact of trauma, it's a guide to evolving sexually with your partner, keeping your sex life satisfying, and knowing when it might be time to seek help from a couples therapist.

The Importance of Intimacy

Intimacy is a fundamental aspect of relationships. Issues in this area can lead to dissatisfaction and even contribute to the breakdown of a partnership. Intimacy expands beyond physical closeness: it encompasses feeling safe, fully open, and connected with one's partner, even in non-physical moments. A healthy relationship thrives on mutual respect, open communication, and genuine care for each other's needs.

With sexual desire, it's essential to recognize the distinction between spontaneous and responsive desire. While some people may experience an immediate urge for sex, others may require external cues to ignite desire. Stress, feelings of isolation, or being overwhelmed can hinder responsive desire, emphasizing the need for understanding and support from partners.

Addressing intimacy issues often involves hard conversations with open communication and may lead you to seek couples therapy, especially when challenges arise in the bedroom. However, improving intimacy and relationships goes beyond addressing sexual concerns; it requires fostering connection through shared experiences and effective communication.

Non-verbal cues and intimate activities can enhance anticipation and pleasure, contributing to a more satisfying sexual experience. However, it's important to note that non-verbal cues might be challenging for neurodivergent individuals, who may require more explicit communication to understand their partner's needs and responses.

```
Staying present is crucial during sex.
Being mindful of the current moment
connects you and your partner during
intimate moments. Now is truly all you
have. Take advantage of it by noticing
your senses and noticing all that's around
you.
```

Sometimes over-reliance on porn can hinder genuine connection as well. Entertainment can be great, but when it becomes necessary to get the job done, it might be time to take a look at your relationship to porn. Make sure to have open conversations about your feelings about porn.

Redefining sex as "pleasure" can alleviate performance pressure and encourage exploration in various ways to experience satisfaction together. Understanding common misconceptions about sexual experiences, such as unrealistic expectations or the belief that discussing sex indicates a problem, is essential for promoting a healthy sexual connection within a relationship.

Setting expectations in your relationship can be a double-edged sword, as it may inadvertently lead to disappointment and resentment. When you have rigid expectations about how the relationship should unfold, you risk overlooking the fluidity and evolution inherent in human connection. Unrealistic or uncommunicated expectations can create tension and misunderstandings, as you both may interpret the other's actions through your own predetermined lens. Excessive emphasis on meeting specific expectations can overshadow the spontaneity and authenticity that enrich intimate bonds. Instead of fixating on predetermined outcomes, you both can benefit from fostering open dialogue, flexibility, and a willingness to adapt to each other's changing needs and desires. When we do this, we promote mutual understanding, acceptance, and a deeper connection, ultimately fostering a more fulfilling and resilient relationship.

Many of us carry the weight of past trauma, which often silently scripts the way we interact with our partners, particularly in moments of closeness and touch. Trauma isn't just a lifeless relic of the past; it breathes in the present, shapes our desires and responses, and directly affects our ability to connect. Maybe you have heard that "the body keeps the score" or how trauma can manifest as a sudden flashback during an intimate moment or as a subtle tense-ness when touch is offered or received.

Establishing safety becomes paramount. A safe space where flashbacks are not just recognized but are understood and validated. In this space, communication takes on the sacred role of careful navigation and gentle exploration.

In therapy, you can begin to unravel your individual narratives—those quiet echoes of trauma that might be intertwined with physical closeness. You can peel back the layers of what has been unsaid, perhaps for years, and directly address it with tenderness. Therapy can serve as a bridge back to yourself and to your partner, giving you a physical space for both healing and reconnection.

For someone with a history of trauma, the approach to intimacy might need a new framework—perhaps a sexual menu, which we will discuss later in this book. If we craft experiences that acknowledge the survivor's autonomy while fostering shared moments of vulnerability, survivors can enjoy pleasurable, safe sex.

```
Our narrative isn't a linear one; it bends
and curves around our individual histories
and healing processes. Yet, it's threaded
with the universal truth that our capacity
to give and receive love, in all its
forms, can flourish, even in the tender
places where our scars reside.
```

Ultimately, if we prioritize our sexual connection, maintain a strong relationship foundation, build autonomy and safety, and challenge societal norms surrounding sexuality, we will be better equipped to sustain a fulfilling and intimate partnership.

Why Sex Gets Harder the Longer You're Together

It's a common misconception that sexual satisfaction is directly tied to the duration of a relationship and the level of love and intimacy between partners. Contrary to popular belief, the quality of sexual relations often decreases over time in couples who still love each other. Sexual satisfaction decreases as relationships progress, with couples having sex less frequently and feeling less satisfied with their sex lives.

People also tend to no longer seduce or desire their partner the longer they are together. People say, "I have needs," and there is a difference between having needs and desiring your partner and seducing them to have sex with them. That's what keeps the spark alive, so it's not monotonous. However, this decline in sexual satisfaction is not inevitable. If we can understand the reasons behind this trend and take proactive steps to maintain a healthy sex life, we can prevent or reverse this decline.

Do you ever worry that things might never be like they were at the beginning?

Several factors contribute to the decline in sexual satisfaction over time, including the routine and predictability of long-term relationships, the decrease in novelty and excitement, the impact of stress, children, and other life changes, and the decline in communication and emotional intimacy.

Novelty is one of the most important factors in keeping our interest and excitement. When we are surprised or thrilled by taboo, it can lead to some hot interactions. By continuously desiring and seducing our partners, we can keep the relationship dynamic and exciting, fostering a deeper emotional and physical connection.

Life can get in the way of prioritizing your sexual connection. When times are busy, pleasure falls by the wayside. Sometimes the time of day matters as well. Some people are more into sex in the morning and some people only ever want to get it on at night. Make sure to have candid conversations about your ideal time for sex and context you want it to happen in.

Intentionally nurturing your connection with your partner is a must, as ignoring this leads to emotional distance that can chip at the foundation of your relationship. You have to carve out moments from the whirlwind of daily life to prioritize the pulse of your relationship. If you can find joy in the unexpected and the unexplored or the simplicity of new conversation, you might find your next chat deep into the excitement of untried fantasies and desires.

Having these open and heartfelt conversations, where you both address the undercurrents of stress, anxiety, or unresolved issues in your lives will transform your potential fights into hard but efficient conversations. Going into a hard conversation can feel so stressful, but getting through it with each other will provide you both with so much relief.

> Several factors that contribute to the decline in sexual satisfaction over time:
>
> - Routine and predictability of long-term relationships
> - Decrease in novelty and excitement
> - Impact of stress, children, and other life changes
> - Decline in communication and emotional intimacy

Sex Therapy

Sex therapy has become more recognized in recent years, emerging to address the gaps in traditional psychology's approach to sexuality. Historically, sexuality has been a taboo topic, but now there's a movement toward treating it holistically, incorporating physical health, pleasure, and emotion. Critics argue that sex therapy often marginalizes individuals by treating sex as a separate issue rather than integrating it into general therapy.

The field faces significant challenges due to the lack of standardized training for therapists. Only Florida has state licensure for sex therapy, while other states lack such requirements, leading to inconsistencies in the quality of care. Organizations like the American Association of Sexuality Educators, Counselors, and Therapists (AASECT) are working to standardize training, but the process is costly and time-consuming. This lack of standardization negatively impacts clients, particularly marginalized populations who already face barriers to accessing mental health services.

Sex education in the United States is also problematic, often relying on fear-based tactics that are counterproductive. Comprehensive, evidence-based sex education that emphasizes the pleasures of sex is needed to combat the misinformation spread by sources like pornography.

Sex therapy is essential because it addresses the deep-seated shame and negative attitudes many people, especially women, have about their sexuality due to cultural and religious influences. By shifting the focus from shame to a sex-positive model, therapists can provide more effective care (Sheffer, 2018).

The field of sex therapy is still developing, and much more research is needed to establish it as a widely accepted form of treatment. Standardization, better training programs, and increased funding for research are crucial for the future growth of sex therapy.

How Sexuality Works

Authentic sexual well-being stems from confidence and joy, which come from knowing the truth about one's body, sexuality, and internal experience and loving what's true. Contrary to popular belief, frequency or constant physical attraction are not the key factors in maintaining a strong sexual connection. Instead, couples who prioritize sex and have a strong foundation of friendship built on trust tend to sustain a fulfilling sexual relationship.

The main reason that most couples seek sex therapy is often differences in pleasure rather than a mismatched desire. For instance, one partner may find pleasure through slow, sensual, emotional intimacy while the other may seek more spontaneous, novel, and physical interactions. This difference in how pleasure is experienced and expressed can lead to misunderstandings and dissatisfaction within the relationship. While exploring individual experiences of lust, play, care, and seeking space can help you understand each other's sexuality more deeply. Remember, desire works differently for everyone.

Do you ever find yourself wishing you could feel desire again?

Libido is strange. You can be all in – pedal to the metal – but if your foot is also on the brake, you're not going anywhere. You can "want to want it" but this isn't always enough. This can be like when you're feeling ready to be intimate, but something inside you, maybe worries or unresolved feelings, are slamming on your brakes. It could be your worries but sometimes it's a distraction. A tug-of-war where you want to move forward but can't. Understanding why this is happening is key to figuring out those moments when, despite being entirely up for it, something is just blocking you. Many struggle with excessive stimulation of their brakes, which factors like worry, insecurity, or cultural messages can trigger. Creating a low-stress, high-affection, and high-trust context is critical to interpreting the world as a pleasurable, safe, and sexy place. It's about finding that sweet spot and easing up on the brake while hitting the gas.

The Dual Control Model

An important concept to understand is the brain's Dual Control Model, which regulates sexual response, and is needed for improving sexual functioning. Our desire and arousal depend on the balance between sexual excitation and sexual inhibition.

Think of your sexual response like driving a car with an accelerator and a brake pedal. The accelerator is all about what turns you on and gets you going, while the brake pedal represents what slows down or stops your sexual arousal. This idea, called the Dual Control Model, highlights how everyone's sexual responses are a mix of go and stop signals, shaped by our unique biology, personal experiences, and psychological factors. It's a useful way to understand why what works for one person in terms of getting turned on might not work for someone else, and how each of us navigates our own sexual desires and inhibitions.

We all have different sexual personalities, influenced by our aforementioned unique "gas pedal" and "brakes" in the brain. This is a metaphor coined by sex educator, Dr. Emily Nagoski. She explains that sexual experience depends heavily on context, and what feels exciting or annoying can change based on the situation. Stress is a significant sex killer, and it's important to find healthy outlets to express stress before engaging in sexual activity. Pop culture, especially media portrayals of women, can negatively impact body image and sexual experiences, perpetuating unrealistic standards and insecurities.

DO'S AND DONT'S

DUAL CONTROL MODEL

DO:
- Experimentation and exploration
- Self-care

DO:
- Open communication
- Stress Reduction

DON'T
- Invalidate yourself
- Self-neglect

DON'T
- Silent treatment
- Overstimulate

The Dual Control Model, or the "go" system and the "stop" system, tell us when to be cautious or hold back and are influenced by what you find attractive or what makes us feel worried or unsafe. This explains why some of us have different reactions to sexual cues and situations. Originally, it helped researchers understand why some people might take more risks with their sexual behavior or face challenges with sexual activity. Now, it's also used to understand a wider range of sexual behaviors and feelings, including why some people experience intense sexual desires or none at all.

Commonly shared advice on boosting your libido often tells you to increase what turns you on, like wearing sexy lingerie or reading romance novels. But, this misses half the story—your "sexual brakes," or the things that turn you off or slow down your desire. To truly tap into your sexual excitement, it's crucial to identify what's hitting your brakes, like stress or body image concerns, and learn how to ease off them. Finding balance means not just ramping up the excitement but also understanding and managing what holds you back. Techniques like stress reduction, open communication with your partner, and building self-esteem can help you moderate these brakes. By addressing both what turns you on and what turns you off, you'll be better positioned to enjoy a fulfilling sexual experience.

Understanding these two systems can help us see that our sexual responses are very personal. They can change based on many factors, like our mood, the situation we're in, or our past experiences. There's a lot of variation in how people experience and respond to sexual attraction and activities.

Navigating what activates your desire and what dampens it can significantly enhance your sexual experiences. Arousal is not solely about amplifying what turns you on, but also identifying your "sexual brakes," like stress or body image issues. Some of us have extremely sensitive brakes! To truly engage with your sexual excitement, identifying and managing these inhibitory factors is crucial. People on the Ace or Asexual spectrum may have overly sensitive brakes compared to Allosexual people. Allosexual is an LGBTQIA+ term for people who experience sexual attraction to others and do not identify as asexual.

Responsive Desire

There's also responsive desire, which emerges in anticipation of pleasure or in response to it, plays a crucial role in maintaining a strong sexual connection. Couples who prioritize sexual connection, even in the face of difficult feelings or distractions, can nurture this form of desire. Addressing underlying emotional distance or difficult feelings between partners is essential for promoting a healthy sexual relationship. We will come back to this soon.

Some people hear the word 'sex' and instantly are ready for action, while others might not be as responsive. Being physically turned on doesn't always mean you're actually into it. If you have experienced trauma, sexual-harm, or had non-consensual past experiences, there is a need for open conversations about what's truly satisfying, safe words, and ways you express discomfort in the moment. Safe words, widely used in Kink/BDSM communities, are essential for clear communication and safety for people who have experienced sexual harm. For those unfamiliar with Kink/BDSM, the simple Red/Yellow/Green system is an easy-to-understand introduction to safe words and their importance. Green signifies that the parties involved are enjoying the activity, and the play can continue. Yellow signifies that the play needs to slow down, that the individual needs a minute, and to continue the play with caution. Red signifies a FULL STOP, meaning the play must cease immediately. Oftentimes, porn doesn't show real experiences like negotiating safewords and boundaries or experiencing pain or discomfort during sex.

The way sex and sexuality are shown in the media often sets us up for false expectations and body image issues, leading to insecurities and myths that make it difficult to enjoy ourselves. Due to overly thin women and muscular men being at the forefront of these false expectations, finding displeasure in your body will definitely get in the way of sex and make it hard to be present or enjoy. Learning to love yourself and improving how you see your body can make a huge difference in enjoying sex and feeling good in general. Realizing that involuntary reactions during unwanted sexual encounters don't reflect your real desires or intentions is key to understanding and healing. Misunderstandings about sex can cause a lot of stress and confusion, but sexuality is complex, and with empathy, honest conversations, and understanding, you can alleviate your concerns and find more pleasure in your life.

When it comes to sexual desire, know that the kind of spontaneity that you see in movies isn't what keeps a long-term sexual connection going. It's sexy to watch, maybe even get you in the mood, but not always real life. Embracing ideas like responsive desire and maybe even planning when to get intimate can actually help keep the spark alive. Scheduling sex can be sexy! The myth that sex should always be spontaneous makes us feel inadequate and less than when it's predictable, familiar, or, god forbid, scheduled. Setting aside time creates intentionality and routine.

In your long-term relationship, it is normal to wish you felt more excited about being intimate—not just going through the motions, but really craving connection. It's not that you want to force yourself to feel something you don't; rather, desire can grow and change over time. If you are waiting for that sudden spark, you might be waiting a while—life gets busy. Consider how building intimacy and exploring new experiences together can gradually ignite that desire. It's about looking at your relationship and finding paths to rediscover excitement, showing that passion doesn't have to fade but can evolve in new and unexpected ways.

Since desire doesn't always come first, getting into the action can spark the feelings and lead to arousal. It's like not realizing you're hungry until you start eating. Instead of waiting for desire to spontaneously ignite, engaging in intimate moments—even if you're not initially feeling it—can often kickstart that feeling. This encourages you to actively explore what triggers your desire, taking control of your sexual experiences. When you experiment and understand your own responses, you're not just passively waiting for desire but rather you're actively inviting it in, making your sexual journey more about discovery and less about waiting for the right moment. It's essential to recognize that experiencing a shift towards responsive desire over time is entirely normal and does not indicate any deficiency in one's sexual well-being. It's normal for this shift to happen in long-term relationships especially when you are stressed.

Societal norms often prioritize spontaneous desire, this forces the concept that constant wanting is the ideal state for everyone. However, embracing responsive desire as an enjoyable aspect of intimacy can lead to a more fulfilling sexual experience. Knowing that your partner might need help with initiation can help break old patterns. For some people that arousal comes first and triggers desire, and there are many motivations for having sex other than feeling like it.

Putting pleasure at the center of your definition of sexual well-being, rather than desire, will improve your sexual satisfaction. Sex is more than a recreational activity and it meets critical psychological and relational needs. A good sex life can act as a buffer against the drop in relationship satisfaction over time. And so, finding ways to trigger desire is necessary to keep desire alive in long-term partnerships.

Hormones

Hormones also obviously play a role in our sexuality. Many of us know that women's hormone levels change throughout the month, but testosterone levels also fluctuate in a person's body, affecting desire and arousal levels. These hormonal cycles—either spanning a 28-day period or following a daily rhythm—play a significant role in our experiences of intimacy and connection. Mood swings and shifts in sexual desire are commonly changing day to day or hour to hour.

Testosterone levels peak in the morning, leading to the commonly observed morning arousal we call "morning wood", formally known as nocturnal penile tumescence (NPT) (UCI Health, 2023). Desire can differ from moment to moment but sometimes can be predictable or expected at certain times. It's important to remember our physical bodies and how we feel about them, influence our emotional connections, deepest desires and fears, and the way we relate to one another. Understanding these natural cycles gives you deeper empathy and understanding of how all of our bodies work.

Misunderstandings and disagreements often stem from underlying emotional pain and the need for connection, a lot of times, sexual connection. You can foster a healthier relationship by improving your sexual communication by being vulnerable and expressing your needs directly. If you routinely experience fear or anxiety during conflicts, you could benefit from practicing emotional regulation skills by yourself or with a therapist. When you are able to show your appreciation and give each other the benefit of the doubt you also promote a stronger bond between y'all as partners.

The Role of Orgasm

Sex is not a pass-or-fail test, but when we are concerned with orgasm, we lose sight of what pleasure is. Imagine your sexual experiences as a journey in a car. This journey isn't always about speeding along at 70 mph on the open highway; sometimes, you find yourself in bumper-to-bumper traffic, taking leisurely joyrides, or simply parked, enjoying an audiobook under the stars.

Just as these varied driving experiences enrich your journey, sexual experiences extend far beyond the narrow lane of hardcore penetrative sex. Penetrative sex tends to be viewed as something that's mainly for cisgender men, since it focuses a lot on friction that helps them reach ejaculation. But this kind of view doesn't really take into account what people with vaginas need—they often require more than just penetration to really enjoy sex. It's important to broaden our conversation about sex to include these differences, so we're really covering all the bases of what intimacy can mean for different people.

These bases encompass a spectrum of intimacies and pleasures, from the gentle exploration of each other's desires to the slow build-up of emotional connection, akin to a scenic drive through changing landscapes. Embracing the diversity in our sexual experiences is like appreciating the full range of journeys your car can take you on, each with its own pace, scenery, and destinations, contributing to a richer, more fulfilling, and pleasurable adventure.

Focusing solely on the destination of orgasm overlooks the richness of the journey. Inviting playfulness, grace, and curiosity into your intimate moments opens a world of exploration and connection, where the experience itself becomes the real reward.

Fantasy & Desire

Have you ever wondered if what you fantasize about in your head means that you really want to do it in real life? Dr. Justin Lehmiller, a prominent researcher from the Kinsey Institute—a renowned center for the study of gender, sexuality, and relationships—has explored the connections between individuals' fantasies and various aspects of their personalities, attachment styles, and past sexual experiences.

His findings suggest that individuals who are open about their fantasies and act upon them tend to report having the most fulfilling sex lives and relationships. It's important to explore and express one's sexual desires and fantasies within the context of a trusting and understanding relationship. When you embrace and incorporate fantasies into your sexual experiences, you and your partner may enhance your intimacy, satisfaction, and overall relationship quality.

It's important to acknowledge that sexual fantasies involving non-consensual scenarios, such as those involving force or dominance, are not uncommon among trauma survivors, particularly those who have experienced childhood sexual abuse (CSA). Research suggests that survivors of CSA may develop sexual fantasies that reflect elements of their past trauma, including themes of power dynamics and control. Some people may find healthy and consensual ways to act out these fantasies by using role play to engage in what is called "consensual-non-consensual" play. This type of play can be a part of a kink scene for some. Keep in mind that not everyone who has CNC fantasies developed these interests or kinks because of past sexual trauma - our desires and fantasies are complicated, and we can't always tell where they came from!

"These fantasies can serve as a coping mechanism or a way to process past experiences."

It's essential to approach these fantasies with empathy and understanding, recognizing that they do not reflect the survivor's desires for real-life non-consensual encounters but can serve as a coping mechanism. Therapy and support can help survivors navigate their sexual fantasies in a safe and healthy manner, without judgment or shame.

Sexual Blueprints

The Erotic Blueprints™ was created by somatic sexologist Miss Jaiya to help individuals and couples discover and examine their sexual preferences. Read though the blueprints and see what you and your partner(s) relate to.

Energetic:
You love suspense, anticipation, and teasing, and have a sensitivity to sexual energy. You may find pleasure in non-contact play and the emotional connections that happen before physical contact.

Sensual:
You like indulging all of your senses in intimate situations. You take great pleasure in creating the ideal environment with mood-enhancing components like textures, lighting, and music.

Sexual:
You like more straightforward manifestations of sexuality. You may value having an orgasm as a crucial component of sexual fulfillment and frequently place a high value on physical appearance and obvious arousal.

Kinky:
You take pleasure in the unusual. Role-playing, power dynamics, or other unconventional, forbidden, or novel sexual practices may be involved. You may get pleasure from the psychological or physical aspects of kink.

Shapeshifter:
You embody malleability and change. You are able to appreciate a wide range of activities but also need ingenuity from their partners in order to feel completely fulfilled. They are insatiably curious in complexity and variation in their sexual encounters.

Understanding each other's blueprint can improve your communication about your true desires and get you to have more fulfilling sex. Integrating both physical and emotional sensations can spice up your sex life and show you your body's somatic role in sexual health and pleasure.

Prompt for Reflection

Take some time to sit down with yourself or your partner and rank the five blueprints.

- Are there any blueprints that were interesting or new for you to learn about?
- Which blueprints do you feel fit you or your partner.
- Are you interested in trying anything new?
- How can you incorporate this new information about your sexual selves into your relationship?

Sexual Trauma

A positive and respectful approach to sexuality and sexual relationships, encompasses the possibility of having pleasurable and safe sexual experiences, free of coercion, discrimination, and violence. Yet, for those who have endured sexual trauma, achieving this state can seem like a distant reality.

Sexual trauma—be it through abuse, assault, or rape—shatters the very foundation of an individual's ability to engage in and enjoy healthy sexual experiences. Such trauma is often the result of non-consensual coercion, where consent was ambiguous or absent, leaving lasting scars that may deeply affect one's sexual and emotional health. This violation of one's sexual rights disrupts the potential for healthy intimacy and can have pervasive effects on various aspects of life.

Notably different from other forms of interpersonal abuse, sexual trauma uniquely attacks an individual's sexuality, intertwining feelings of love with exploitation and assault. This can significantly impair the ability to form and maintain intimate relationships, creating troublesome, often unconscious associations between abuse dynamics and sexual thoughts, feelings, body parts, and behavior.

In vanilla partnerships, consent and its nuances are often not discussed thoroughly, leading to many boundary violations. In contrast, those who engage in Kink/BDSM place consent at the forefront of every conversation, emphasizing its importance. This is why Kink and BDSM can be a reparative tool for trauma survivors.

Sex therapist Wendy Maltz highlights the extensive impact sexual trauma can have on one's attitudes about sex. Survivors may come to view sex as dirty, view it as a duty, or develop beliefs that they are somehow flawed or damaged sexually. These negative beliefs include feelings that sex is uncontrollable, or that in sexual encounters, one person must dominate. Such distorted perceptions can lead to automatic reactions to touch and intimacy, where survivors might feel panic, fear, or even act out sexually in ways that can be harmful to themselves and others (Maltz, 2002).

Techniques like sensate focus, which involves taking sex off the table to focus on non-sexual touching and gradually reintroducing non-penetrative sexual elements, help survivors take incremental steps back into the realm of intimate connection without feeling overwhelmed. I usually tell couples early on in therapy that they are "not allowed" to have sex, (forbidden!) and need to explore the other options for pleasure. This method emphasizes mutual understanding and careful processing of emotions, allowing both partners to explore their needs and boundaries safely.

Many of the various therapy modalities such as EMDR (Eye Movement Desensitization and Reprocessing), and IFS (Internal Family Systems) along with somatic experiencing, offer frameworks for addressing and healing from sexual trauma. These approaches help you reconnect with your body, manage your emotional responses, and ultimately restore those vital connections to yourself and others that trauma has disrupted.

Recovering from the wounds of trauma goes beyond overcoming pain; it's also about rediscovering the capacity to feel pleasure, joy and connection in relationships. Trauma specialist Peter Levine notes trauma is fundamentally about broken connections—between the body, self, family, community, and beyond. Thus, the healing process centers on repairing these bonds, empowering survivors not to recover but to flourish in their relationships and intimate experiences.

While I may not be able to change what my clients go through and take away their pain with a magic wand, I can guide them to a new vantage point where they can reframe their story—a view where the canyon looks vastly different from above looking down, than it does from below looking up. A shift in our perspective is vital because it transforms our narrative from one of victimhood and pain to one of survival and resilience. In the therapeutic space, we weave new stories, not by denying the past, but by re-authoring the grip it has on our present, stitching new patterns of understanding, acceptance, and growth (Condos, 2020).

Self-Love

I get people in my office who are well into adulthood before they have taken the time to really take a look at their sexuality. Self-pleasure is how we learn about ourselves and our body, so we can know what we want and how to ask for it.

Throughout history, there have been many misconceptions about masturbation that have shaped behaviors and beliefs, at times, leading to some unusual dietary recommendations. Bland foods like unsweetened Kellogg's Corn Flakes® were meant to curb the urge to masturbate, a belief widely held by healthcare professionals of the time. Despite advancements in understanding human sexuality, many myths still persist around masturbation, impacting your sexual well-being that causes shame.

Cis women, in particular, may experience shame around masturbation, which can hinder their ability to achieve orgasm with a partner. Conversely, men might develop unhealthy patterns if they rely solely on masturbation for sexual satisfaction. Recognizing the role of masturbation is crucial in addressing sexual issues and dispelling myths that cloud its understanding. It is widely accepted in society for men to masturbate, yet there is often discomfort with the idea of women being sexual beings independently.

Common myths include the belief that people who use vibrators or toys for masturbation will become dependent on them, become numb, or be unable to achieve orgasm by other means. However, by actively exploring your body through masturbation, you can find it easier to attain orgasm with a partner. You can also consider masturbating with your partner! Additionally, it's a misconception that those in relationships masturbate less than single individuals; in reality, relationship status does not significantly influence masturbation habits.

Other myths suggest that cis women primarily masturbate by inserting objects into the vagina, whereas clitoral stimulation is actually more common. Misguided beliefs about early childhood masturbation label it as abnormal or indicative of hypersexuality despite it being a normal and common behavior. Fears that masturbation can lead to adverse health risks or impact performance in sports or physical activities are unfounded; masturbation offers positive health benefits, including stress relief, sleep aid, and improved immune functioning. Lastly, the idea that masturbation causes premature ejaculation or erectile dysfunction is false, highlighting the need for better education and communication regarding this natural aspect of human sexuality.

Changing the narrative and dispelling negativity around masturbation is essential for personal growth, improved sexual health, and better communication. Masturbation is actually healthy and offers numerous health benefits, including: for men*, reducing the risk of prostate cancer, improving sleep, boosting mood, enhancing sperm motility, strengthening erections by exercising the pelvic floor muscles, and reducing premature ejaculation and other sexual issues. For women*, it can also provide advantages such as reducing stress, improving sleep, alleviating menstrual cramps, boosting immunity, strengthening the pelvic floor, addressing sexual problems, and enhancing sexual satisfaction (Grey, 2024). Reflecting on and altering our language around masturbation helps us have a healthier societal perspective, encouraging understanding.

Our self-image is greatly influenced by our body image, which frequently results in self-hatred and limits our ability to form meaningful connections with our partners. We don't want to be naked, and we lose confidence and a sense of worth when we have a negative self-perception. Exercises that boost confidence and positive affirmations are two examples of body image-enhancing activities that can have an empowering effect. Engaging in these activities can make you feel more in control of your bodies and sex, which leads to more satisfying sex. Building a positive self-image helps us to tear down barriers caused by self-doubt and shame, which creates space for more sincere and fulfilling relationships with our partners.

Self-pleasure is a potent tool for boosting self-esteem and improving body image. Self-love enables you to learn about your body, comprehend your desires, and gain a greater appreciation for your physical form. This approach helps us destroy shameful emotions and empower us to have a positive self-image. Your personal well-being and relationships are strengthened and become more intimate and connected when you are comfortable and confident in your own skin. Developing a healthy sense of self requires an understanding of the connection between body image and self-satisfaction.

What's on the Menu

I often recommend the couples I see, including those in queer and non-binary relationships, to create what is called a sexual menu; sometimes called a kink menu. This tool is intended to be inclusive and equally applicable for queer, non-binary, cisgender, and heterosexual couples.

It's a technique that promotes partners to discuss and share their sexual wants, likes, and limits. Picture it as a catalog of shared experiences and adventures that you both are curious about creating. It's an activity for candid discussions about your deepest desires. You might be surprised to know that many couples, some who have even been together for decades, have never even had a real conversation about their desires.

The menu is not one-size-fits-all; it's customizable to fit the unique dynamics of your relationship, whether you need to establish safety, build trust, express vulnerability, or simply inject playfulness into your relationship. It's particularly useful for navigating physical or emotional challenges in intimacy, providing options that respect and reflect the various sexual identities and preferences of everyone involved. It's a fun and innovative way to create moments that prioritize your personal comfort and limits.

Maybe for a person facing the challenge of erectile dysfunction, they would create a menu that doesn't hinge on an erection. Their menu would include everything that could be pleasurable that does not include them being hard.

For individuals working through trauma, their menu might include specific safety measures such as using safe words, establishing clear boundaries prior to any activity, or incorporating soothing music to create a calming environment. These elements help build a setting where they can feel secure and supported, even in challenging moments.

Similarly, if you are dealing with pain upon or during penetration, you could devise a menu that excludes penetration, ensuring sex remains enjoyable and pain-free. Pelvic floor physical therapy can help you externally and internally by massaging and regulating the muscles. (I have seen pelvic floor physical therapy work like magic and helps you feel so much better!).

We can reawaken dormant passions, feel empowered, and explore new dimensions of connection when we have agency, a sense of security, are willing to be open, and when we have *willingness* to want to want it. Cultivating a sense of eroticism and playfulness within the relationship can help with reawakening these passions and the next section includes an exercise that can help you do just that.

The Stopwatch Game

Set a timer for 3 or 5-minute intervals.

Each time the timer goes off, explore what can be done using only certain options. These options could include:

- Using only mouths
- Using only hands
- Keeping eyes closed
- Focusing on a specific body part

The key is to focus on pleasure and intimacy, aiming to bring your partner to their most pleasurable state without pursuing orgasm as the ultimate goal. This exercise encourages creativity, communication, and a deeper connection with your partner, enhancing your overall sexual experience.

What would sex be like if penetration was off the table?

Our Analogous Bodies

The human body isn't as different as it may seem; all genitalia share a common origin through a process called homology. Despite this, every person who is assigned female at birth (AFAB) has a vagina and vulva that is distinct, and the way they are portrayed in porn can create unrealistic expectations about how they should look and function.

It's fascinating to think that we all start from the same blueprint. In those early stages, nestled in the womb, our bodies don't show their cards yet; they're waiting on cues from our genes and the hormone cocktail they're served. This process is what eventually sculpts our diverse anatomies. Interestingly enough, 1-2% of the population, or the same number of people that are born with red hair, are born with sexual ambiguities and might identify as intersex. Intersex refers to individuals who are born with physical sex characteristics that do not fit typical binary notions of male or female bodies. Reflecting on our shared beginnings, it's a reminder of our common humanity, how, beneath the surface, we're not very different after all.

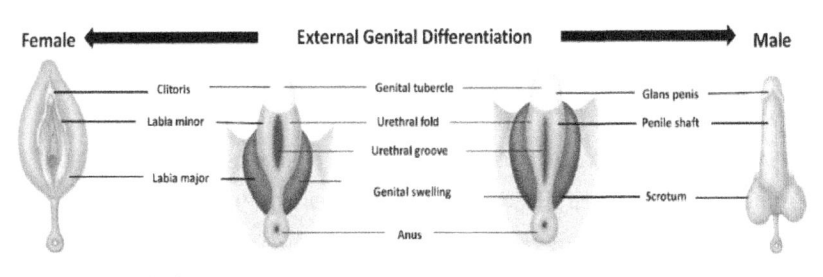

Female ←	External Genital Differentiation	→ Male
Clitoris	Genital tubercle	Glans penis
Labia minor	Urethral fold	Penile shaft
Labia major	Urethral groove	Scrotum
	Genital swelling	
	Anus	

(Flück, 2023)

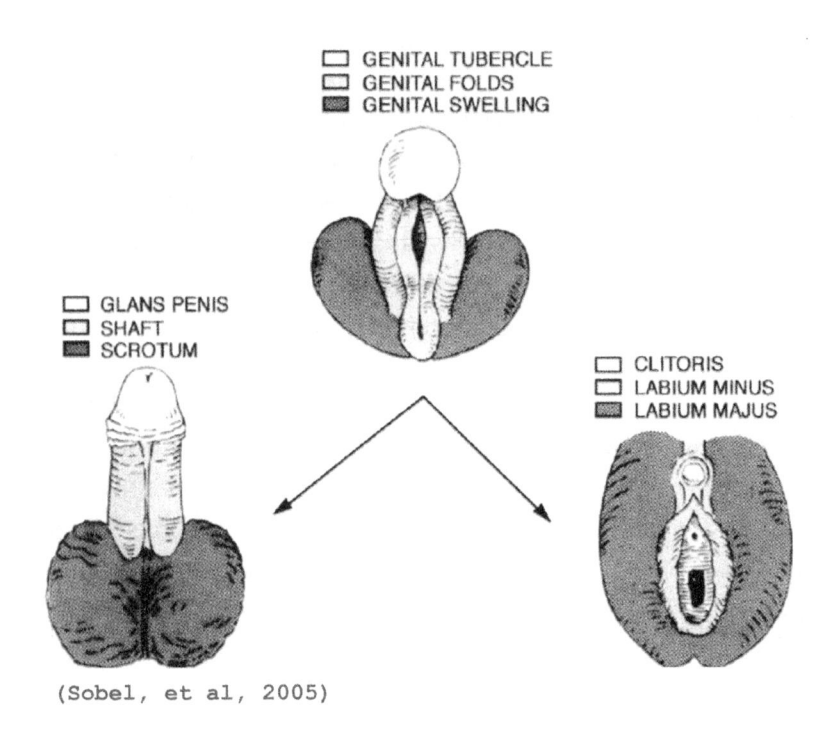

☐ GENITAL TUBERCLE
☐ GENITAL FOLDS
▓ GENITAL SWELLING

☐ GLANS PENIS
☐ SHAFT
▓ SCROTUM

☐ CLITORIS
☐ LABIUM MINUS
▓ LABIUM MAJUS

(Sobel, et al, 2005)

It also might come as a surprise, but the full anatomy of the clitoris wasn't mapped out until the early 2000s. Before this revelation, our understanding and representations, especially in educational settings, grossly underestimated its size and complexity. This discovery isn't just a footnote in medical textbooks; it fundamentally changes how we understand female arousal and pleasure. Realizing the clitoris extends well beyond its visible part, we uncover a whole new landscape dedicated to pleasure. This vast "real estate" challenges and enriches our exploration of intimacy, inviting us to broaden our horizons and deepen our connections.

The Right to Sex

In a society where people promote that sex is for procreation, a lot of men aren't allowed to explore sex and sexuality without fear of being labeled or misunderstood. While it is easier for men to have an orgasm (thanks to friction), many men don't know how to express their needs, desires, and interests.

Men are taught that they need to be protectors; however, they are not allowed to be vulnerable because that shows weakness, and intimacy is seen as "feminine". Therefore, many men don't know how to be intimate for fear of being judged, or having it weaponized.

Often men experience a lack of intimacy, and the only place they feel they can experience it is through sex. Men in their 30s are hitting a record low in sexual activity. Some men wonder if they have a "right to sex," or wish for the decriminalization of sex work as a solution.

However, the focus, should shift towards examining the societal pressures surrounding sex and the noticeable absence of intimacy many men face. Many men hesitate to open up and show vulnerability, which leads to a deeper fear of experiencing closeness without the sexual aspect. Encouraging men to embrace and value intimacy beyond the confines of sex is a vital conversation. This is a deeper, more authentic discussion on the essence of intimacy and affection.

So, do you have a right to sex in your relationship? This question nudges us toward a nuanced exploration of consent, desire, and mutual respect within our partnerships. It's not about claiming a right but fostering an environment where intimacy flourishes through open dialogue, understanding, and mutual desire.

Prioritizing consent and communication establishes a foundation where you both feel seen, valued, and connected, transcending mere physical interaction to a more fulfilling expression of love and intimacy.

The conversation about the right to sex includes people with disabilities. There is a consensus that more education on the topic is important for both healthcare professionals and disabled individuals in order to increase disabled representation (Byra & Żyta, 2018). In these relationships it is important to emphasize communication, awareness of emotions, and consent.

This right to sex is also extended to the elderly. When it comes to the need and desire for intimacy, age is irrelevant. Intimacy, affection, and sex continue to play significant roles in people's lives as they get older. However, due to changes in health and physical state, it may take on a different form and expression.

Making changes in our society, like having better sex education, is important. To guarantee that a person's right to sex is not restricted because of physical changes, information about age-related changes such as menopause and erectile dysfunction, as well as solutions for these issues, should be more accessible.

Acknowledging the shifts that accompany aging, we should also recognize how critical it is to modify our experiences of intimacy and sexuality, just as we adjust to new developments in our health..

`Some ideas for conversations include:`

What can I do to make sure you feel understood?

What does consent look like for us?

What can we explore to make you more comfortable?

Comfortability can come in different forms whether it is a different position, the addition of toys, or BDSM equipment. A Cerebral Palsy comedian Tina Firml (2024) stated that, "I'm not into bondage in that helpless fantasy kinda way. I'm just happy to not be moving."

Keeping your body as comfortable as possible also means knowing when is the best time for you to be intimate. Whether it is after your medication starts working, when you feel the most control over your body, or when your body temperature is the most comfortable, your safety and comfort plays a factor in your sexuality and can help facilitate good communication and creativity in your relationship (Tepper, 2015).

Sometimes, comfort does not seem achievable. When this is the case it is important to seek out a medical health professional first and foremost, but some patients find that chronic pain needs more of a multidisciplinary approach (Meana & Binik, 2022). Multidisciplinary approaches don't just include seeing a doctor, but also a therapist and a physical therapist. Worsley et al. (2016) and Blair et al. (2014) found that;

In both same sex marriages and heterosexual marriages CBT therapy and understanding how to set and uphold your boundaries helped contribute to reducing pain felt during sex.

> *Prompt for Reflection*
>
> Take this time to talk with your partner about their experiences and expectations in the past, exploring narratives that have shaped intimacy and sexual desire.
>
> This conversation is an opportunity to deepen your understanding of each other, highlighting the importance of empathy, patience, and open-mindedness.
>
> You can co-create a space where both of you feel comfortable expressing your needs, fears, and fantasies, fostering a relationship where intimacy is not just about physical closeness but a deep emotional connection.

Challenges with Orgasm

Reaching the climax is often seen as the grand finale, the ultimate goal when arousal kicks in, but it's far from the most important part of the experience. Despite sounding a bit cheesy, the truth is that sex becomes truly thrilling and filled with playfulness and curiosity when the focus extends beyond just the concluding moments. It's the adventure along the way, exploring each turn with eagerness, that truly enriches the experience.

But for many of us, it's not that easy. Facing challenges like prematurely ejaculating or struggling to reach climax can be difficult and disheartening. These experiences can make the journey toward satisfaction feel fraught with hurdles, turning moments meant for connection and enjoyment into sources of frustration or embarrassment. With knowledge about your body and your partner's, navigating these hurdles can become easier. Understanding each other's needs, desires, and the intricacies of how you both experience pleasure paves the way for more fulfilling encounters.

For the Vulva

Maybe you and your friends have debated the differences between clitoral and internal "G-spot" orgasms, not knowing it's a misconception. Research shows us that all orgasms in individuals with vulvas are clitoral, due to the clitoris's extensive network reaching around the pelvic area, including the vaginal walls. What are often labeled as different types of orgasms are, in fact, variations of clitoral stimulation.

The clitoris is a lush hub of pleasure, packed with thousands of nerve fibers — more than any other part of the body. Researchers believe that the Clitoris has more nerve endings than previously known; the mean number of myelinated nerve fibers innervating the clitoris was 10,281, ranging from 9,852 to 11,086 (Uloko et al,. 2023). This dense network of nerves makes it exceptionally sensitive, marking it as a vast erogenous zone perfect for exploration.

Most people are familiar with the small bump at the top of the vulva, but it is actually a much larger structure; And although the clitoris was identified in the 16th century, it wasn't until the early 21st century that it was seen in its entirety. Healthcare and science has largely overlooked its significance for centuries but more interest in pleasure seems to be changing the tides. The Clitoris is the only organ designed for pleasure alone.

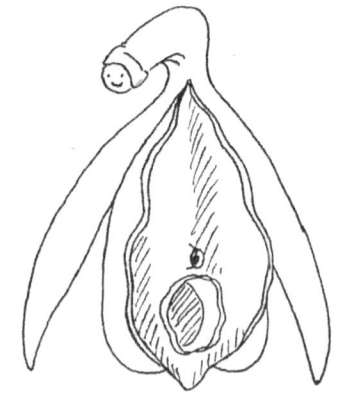

When we understand the full structure of the clitoris, we can understand how to enhance our orgasmic potential, become more orgasmic, and overcome orgasm challenges.

Knowing the extensive physical space dedicated to pleasure allows you to mentally and physically access it more effectively.

Many cis women and people with vulvas encounter challenges in achieving internal orgasms during intercourse or what they believe to be internal. Pleasure can manifest in numerous ways, including some that you may not have previously considered. It's crucial to expand our understanding of what pleasure means and to address common misconceptions and misunderstandings surrounding orgasms.

While it doesn't need to be the goal, experimenting with different approaches can enhance the pleasure of intimacy and help you experience orgasm through penetration. It's about discovering what feels good, which might involve playing around with various kinds of pleasure. Being open to exploring and willing to see where these new paths take you can make for some unexpectedly pleasurable experiences alone or with your partner.

Practicing penetrative touch during solo sex is another productive step. Self-exploration allows for a better understanding of how to achieve internal orgasms and what specifically feels good, paving the way for more satisfying penetrative sex.

Addressing physical discomfort is essential for enhancing your sexual experience. If you encounter pain during intercourse, consulting a pelvic floor physical therapist could be a game-changer. Considering that 1 in 10 women deal with endometriosis, pain isn't uncommon for many, but it shouldn't be something you just accept as normal. Listen to your body and seek professional help when needed to ensure both your physical and sexual well-being are in harmony.

Cultivating trust and the ability to surrender plays a significant role in overcoming any mental barriers to orgasm. Learning to let go of fears, anxieties, or concerns that may inhibit orgasm requires developing trust in both your body and your partner, fostering a relaxed and receptive state during intercourse.

Lastly, communication with your partner is essential. Being open and honest about your preferences, what feels good and what doesn't, is vital to a fulfilling sexual experience. Sharing your needs and desires can guide your partner in providing more pleasurable and satisfying experiences during penetrative sex. By embracing these approaches, we can explore and expand our capacity for pleasure during intercourse, opening up new possibilities for orgasmic experiences during penetrative and non-penetrative sex.

For the Penis

Key pelvic muscles, located at the base of the penis, are essential for functions like ejaculation and urinating. Strengthening these muscles can lead to improvements in erectile issues. Here are three beneficial exercises:

- **The 4-8-12-16 Exercise** involves gently squeezing the muscles around the base of the penis. You should aim to hold this squeeze for durations of 4, 8, 12, or 16 seconds before releasing. It's essential to breathe naturally between each set to avoid unnecessary tension.

- **The Child's Pose** with Pelvic Floor Muscle Engagement exercise starts on your hands and knees. As you exhale, move your hips back towards your heels while engaging your pelvic muscles. Inhaling, relax these muscles and return to your starting position. This exercise helps control muscle tension and promote relaxation.

- **T Cat-Cow Pose** with Pelvic Floor muscle engagement begins in a similar hands-and-knees position. With an inhale, arch your back downwards, looking up for the cow pose. Upon exhaling, round your back towards the ceiling, entering the cat pose, and simultaneously squeeze your pelvic muscles. This exercise not only strengthens the pelvic floor but also promotes spinal flexibility.

These exercises are to enhance your pelvic muscle control, increase body awareness, and improve nervous system communication.

Specifically, they can help in managing the autonomic nervous system's response that triggers the shift from erection to ejaculation, potentially enhancing sexual stamina and control.

Ejaculatory issues are relatively common among cis men, with premature ejaculation being one of the most frequently reported issues. Despite its prevalence, a small fraction of affected men seek help, often due to feelings of embarrassment. Premature ejaculation can be categorized as either lifelong, where it occurs very quickly during sexual activity, often within minutes, or acquired, where there's a noticeable decrease in the duration before ejaculation over time a lot of times due to age.

The causes of premature ejaculation can be biological, neurobiological, genetic, or psychological. Treatments differ based on the type of premature ejaculation. Sometimes it includes topical numbing agents, SSRIs known for their potential side effects like reduced sexual desire, and sex therapy that helps to extend ejaculation time.

Opening Up

Maybe you have thought about the idea of dating multiple people, or think it's hot to imagine your partner hooking up with someone else. Polyamorous and open relationships can be healthy and fulfilling for some people, providing opportunities for personal growth, enhanced communication, and a variety of emotional support. However, they can be deeply stressful for others, potentially leading to feelings of jealousy, insecurity, and emotional instability. It's essential to recognize that these relationships are not a one-size-fits-all solution.

Many couples think about opening up their relationship and exploring ethical non-monogamy (ENM)/ consensual non-monogamy (CNM). While I won't go into these topics in depth in this book, I do want to share some important points.

For example, opening a relationship expands the traditional monogamous framework, while polyamory challenges the couple as the main social unit. These terms are often thrown around in everyday language and sometimes misused.

In today's conversations about relationships and therapy, terms like "boundaries" and "attachment styles" come up frequently. However, no single attachment model or theory fully captures the complexities of ENM and CNM.

```
Some people use therapy jargon, boundaries,
and attachment styles to justify hurtful
behaviors, trying to control their partners
in unhealthy ways, such as weaponizing
boundaries or triggers.
```

However, polyamory and community-focused lifestyles can offer significant healing and benefits that go beyond sexual relationships. These lifestyles challenge the idea that intimacy and security can only be found with one person, emphasizing that sometimes one person can't meet all needs, whether in a polyamorous or monogamous context.

If you're considering opening up your relationship, it's important to do your research and consider talking to a couples therapist. Make sure you're not doing it just because your partner wants it or because you're afraid of losing them if you don't. Decisions like these should be based on mutual agreement and understanding, with the emotional well-being and consent of all involved as top priorities.

Evolving Together Sexually

Over the course of your relationship or lifetime, evolving sexually with your partner entails an ever-changing process of learning and adaptation. Natural aging processes range from the appearance of wrinkles to changes in muscle tone and alterations in physical abilities. Even though these changes are inevitable, they can occasionally make us question our sense of self and desirability.

It is possible to rekindle your desire! It takes work and acceptance to stay comfortable in our changing bodies, on our own and with our partners. Building strong communication about evolving needs and desires is essential. This could involve discussing discovering fresh sources of happiness or adapting cherished aspects to suit current requirements. Developing your ongoing practices of rekindling desire will help you maintain and increase your connection over time and bring eroticism and playfulness to the relationship.

This progress has the potential to enhance closeness for a lot of couples. It's an opportunity to explore dimensions of intimacy like focusing on sensuality, emotional bonds, or expressing love through artistic means that don't rely heavily on physical stamina or endurance. By helping partners connect deeply with the joys and moments of the now rather than what was attainable before techniques rooted in mindfulness, such as those applied in sexual activities can also enrich closeness.

Education plays a role as well. Understanding how aging affects responses and changes can shed light on various aspects of sexuality in older adults. This could involve seeking out alternative forms of erotic pleasure that don't focus as much on performance, learning more about using sexual aids, or modifying sexual positions to account for physical constraints.

It is possible to change how couples feel intimacy and make it just as fulfilling sexually as any other phase of life. By embracing these changes together, with compassion and curiosity, as opposed to rejection. The important thing is to keep looking at each other with admiration and desire, understanding that although physical appearances can change, a person's ability to convey love, affection, and sexuality need not.

I enjoyed and highly recommend Esther Perel's book "Mating in Captivity." Many of these ideas are highlighted in the book, such as the necessity of effort, communication, and adapting to sustain a vibrant sexual connection. To maintain the spark of desire, Perel emphasizes the significance of balancing security and mystery and continually rewriting your relationship narrative to keep the fire alive. If we embrace our bodies' changes throughout our lives with curiosity and compassion, we will have more fulfilling sex with our partners.

Aftercare

Aftercare is about taking care of each other physically and emotionally after being intimate, and it's a crucial but often overlooked part of sexual experiences. This whole process includes everything from basic hygiene and post-sex care to deeper, supportive conversations that strengthen your emotional bond. It's about ensuring both of you feel respected, comfortable, and cared for, not just in the heat of the moment but also in the quiet that follows.

Taking care of each other emotionally after sex is as important as the physical side, offering gestures of respect, kindness, and understanding towards your partner, whether it's a long-term relationship or a casual hookup. Aftercare redefines the expectations of casual encounters by emphasizing the need for compassion. I usually recommend that if you are in an open relationship or are poly, to include aftercare when you are rejoining with your partner after an experience with someone else.

Aftercare also allows us to avoid vaginal health challenges, like recurrent Bacterial Vaginosis (BV), that usually includes extra hygiene such as peeing post-sexual activity. Many people think only cis-women or AFAB people (assigned female at birth) should pee after sex, but we should all pee when anything foreign touches our genitals. Adopting practices like these, like staying hydrated and keeping sex toys clean, you can prioritize your self-care.

Maintaining a Satisfying Sex Life in Long-Term Relationships:

• Prioritize and make time for sex
• Keep things fresh and exciting by trying new things, experimenting with different positions, locations, and fantasies
• Communicate openly and honestly about sexual needs and desires
• Address any underlying issues impacting sexual satisfaction, such as stress, anxiety, or relationship problems
• Understand the brain's dual control model of sexual response: the accelerator notices sexually relevant information and sends a "turn on" signal, while the brake notices potential threats and sends a "turn off" signal
• Identify and minimize factors that stimulate the brake to improve sexual functioning
• Create a low-stress, high-affection, and high-trust context to interpret the world as pleasurable, safe, and sexy
• Encourage confidence and joy by knowing the truth about one's body, sexuality, and internal experience
• Prioritize sex and create a "protected space" for it in the relationship, built on a strong foundation of friendship and trust

- Understand the concept of "responsive desire," which emerges in anticipation of pleasure or in response to it, and nurture it consciously

- Address and overcome any emotional distance or difficult feelings between partners

- Choose to prioritize the sexual connection, even when faced with difficult emotions or distractions in life

- Understand that sex is a pleasure-based motivation, allowing for joy and ecstasy without frustration and anger

- Recognize that pleasure, connection, and authentic humanity matter in relationships

- Improve communication by being vulnerable and expressing needs directly

- Practice emotional regulation skills, such as using an emotion chart, to manage reactive or withdrawn behaviors during conflicts

- Show appreciation and give each other the benefit of the doubt to promote a healthier relationship

Looking back on how you've grown reading this book, I want you to recognize the progress you've made and the obstacles you've conquered.

Through this experience you've come to understand the significance of communication, intimacy and empathy in your relationship.

As you move forward remember to maintain these values and set goals, for nurturing your bond and stay curious about each other's changing wants and needs. Remember you are the author of your narrative.

If you both prioritize your connection and apply the wisdom shared in this book you can ensure that your relationship not just survives, but thrives.

Should Y'all Go to Couples Therapy?

We've covered a lot of ground on all the ways you can strengthen your connection with your partner. Looking back on how you've grown reading this book, it's important to recognize the progress you've made and the obstacles you've conquered.

Through your experiences you've come to understand the significance of communication, intimacy and empathy in your relationship. As you move ahead remember to maintain these values set goals, for nurturing your bond and stay curious about each other's changing wants and needs.

If you've tried some of the concepts in this book and still feel stuck, it might be time to consider therapy.

A therapist can offer deeper insights and more focused help. Starting your search with someone specialized in couples or sexual health could be your next best step.

Some couples will just read this book. You might want to be guided by your own couples therapist. In the (usually) intricate journey of finding the right therapist for couples counseling, there are crucial considerations to weigh. Whether you're finding therapy for the first time or seeking a new fit, the quest for finding the right therapist for you will be significant in shaping how therapy ends up working for you. However, navigating this process can feel overwhelming, so here are some key factors to consider.

```
Effective communication, fostering emotional
connection,   and   skillfully   repairing
conflicts are essential elements that will
sustain and strengthen your relationship's
foundation.
```

When trying to decide to start therapy, take a moment to reflect on your shared goals you might have. Consider the specific areas you want to address, from relationship dynamics to individual concerns like stress management or identity exploration. Think about whether certain characteristics, such as the therapist's gender or identity, hold significance for you in fostering a comfortable therapeutic environment.

Next, explore the various therapy modalities available and how they align with your preferences. Each therapist brings their unique approach, from Cognitive Behavioral Therapy (CBT), to Psychodynamic, to Dialectical Behavioral Therapy (DBT), to Emotionally-Focused Therapy (EFT) to Narrative Therapy; focusing on one of these theories could impact how your therapy could look. The right modality can help you in selecting a therapist who resonates with your therapeutic goals and values. *(Don't worry, there's more information and a step by step guide coming up next.)*

Seek recommendations from trusted sources, such as friends, family, or healthcare providers, to garner insights into potential therapists who match your needs. Once you've compiled a list of candidates, look into their backgrounds, specialties, and therapy approaches through their website, therapy directories, or initial (sometimes free) consultations.

As you narrow down your options, consider scheduling initial, usually free, consultations to gauge rapport and alignment with potential therapists. Many therapists offer free 15-25 minute initial consultations. These meetings offer invaluable opportunities to ask questions, share concerns, and assess the therapist's suitability for your needs. Trust your instincts and prioritize finding a therapist with whom you feel genuinely heard and supported.

Research consistently emphasizes the critical role of the therapist-client relationship in determining the success of therapy.

This rapport serves as the cornerstone of the therapeutic journey, fostering trust, empathy, and collaboration between therapist and client.

Studies indicate that when clients feel understood and supported by their therapists, they are more engaged in therapy and achieve better outcomes.

Additionally, a strong therapeutic alliance helps address challenges and maintains progress throughout the treatment process. Many people feel like their therapist could be their good friend if circumstances were different. By prioritizing the establishment of a positive relationship, therapists can create a conducive environment for growth and healing in their clients' lives.

Regarding the financial aspect of therapy, deciding whether to use insurance involves weighing various factors. Some individuals opt for out-of-pocket payment to maintain confidentiality, access a broader range of therapists, or address specific therapy modalities or issues not covered by insurance. On the other hand, utilizing insurance may offer financial assistance but could entail limitations on therapist choice or confidentiality concerns. Your therapist will need to give you a diagnosis to use insurance and justify medical necessity.

Navigating online therapy directories can further streamline your search process, with platforms like Psychology Today and GoodTherapy offering comprehensive databases of therapists' profiles and specialties. By leveraging these resources and taking proactive steps towards finding the right therapist, you're on a transformative journey towards personal growth and relational well-being.

Remember, the decision to seek therapy is a courageous act of self-care, and by taking that initial step, you're prioritizing your mental and emotional well-being. Embrace the discomfort, trust your instincts, and rest assured that you're moving towards a brighter, more fulfilling future. Making that first call is often the scariest part, but once you connect with someone you can trust, the process becomes more manageable. Every therapist has a different modality and guiding star for therapy, so it's crucial to find one whose theory aligns with your values and preferences. With persistence and patience, you'll find the perfect therapist for you and your partner, paving the way for healing, growth, and greater relational harmony.

```
All of this information is listed in the
following sections.
```

Appendix - Now What?

Whether you are finding a therapist for the first time or looking for your next perfect couple's therapist, finding the perfect fit for therapy is an important step in your therapy journey. But it can be daunting to start the process. So, here are some things to consider.

What to Consider When Looking for a Couple's Therapist

1. Take some time to reflect on what you hope to achieve through therapy. When searching for a therapist, there are a few things to think about. Consider the specific areas you want to work on, such as managing stress, improving relationships, identity concerns, relationship issues, anxiety, and depression. Would the gender of the therapist matter to you? What about their identity or if they work with people like you?

2. Next, think about the type of therapy that might work best for you, like talking about your thoughts and feelings or learning new coping skills. Every therapist has a different modality and does therapy differently. I work from a Narrative perspective and use Feminist theory to inform the care of the client. It's important to find a therapist who specializes in the specific issue you want to work on, as well as someone you can really trust and get along with. Will it be important for your therapist to understand your background and culture?

3. Seek recommendations from the people around you in your community. Reach out to trusted friends, family members, or colleagues who have had positive experiences with therapy. They may be able to recommend a therapist who aligns with your needs. Additionally, you can ask your primary care physician or search online directories for therapists in your area (which we will go into!) .

4. Once you have a list of potential therapists, take the time to research them. Visit their websites, read their bios, and learn about their areas of expertise. You can also search for online reviews or testimonials to get a sense of other clients' experiences with the therapist.

5. Different therapists may use different approaches, or modalities, in their practice. Research different therapy modalities, such as cognitive-behavioral therapy (CBT), narrative, DBT, ACT, psychodynamic therapy, or mindfulness-based therapy, to see which resonates with you. There are a lot, but don't let this overwhelm you (we will briefly go over this in a couple sections). This can help you narrow down your search to therapists who specialize in the modalities that align with your preferences.

6. Schedule initial consultations! As mentioned, many therapists offer free initial consultations or phone/video calls to discuss your needs and determine if they are a good fit for you. Take advantage of these consultations to ask questions, share your concerns, and get a sense of the therapist's approach and personality. This can help you gauge if you feel comfortable and connected with the therapist before you Invest any money.

Trust your gut and choose someone you feel comfortable talking to. It can be weird talking to a stranger, but that doesn't always mean it will remain that way, it can evolve, just like any relationship it takes a minute, especially when we are talking about sex. But a lot of times if it feels weird in the beginning, it will probably feel weird along the way, and it will be harder for you to want to switch therapists because you won't want to start over.

`Take your time and find someone who makes you feel heard, understood, and supported.`

Don't be afraid to try out a few therapists before making a decision. The right therapist is out there, and together, you can embark on a transformative journey towards personal growth and well-being.

To Use Insurance or Not

When deciding whether to use insurance for therapy or not, there are several factors to consider. Here are some reasons why someone might choose not to use insurance for therapy:

1. `Confidentiality:` When you use insurance, your therapy sessions may be documented in your medical records, which could potentially be accessed by insurance companies or other healthcare providers. Some individuals prefer to keep their therapy completely confidential and choose to pay out-of-pocket to maintain their privacy.

2. `Limited Choice of Therapists:` Insurance plans often have a network of approved therapists, and you may be limited to choosing from within that network. This can restrict your options and make it challenging to find a therapist who aligns with your specific needs and preferences.

3. `Lack of Coverage for Certain Modalities or Issues:` Insurance plans may not cover certain therapeutic modalities or specific issues that you want to address. Some plans may not cover couples therapy or specialized therapies like art therapy or EMDR. Paying out-of-pocket allows you to have more flexibility in choosing the type of therapy that's best for you.

4. `Limited Number of Sessions:` Insurance plans typically have limitations on the number of therapy sessions covered within a certain time frame. If you have complex issues, you may find that the limited coverage is insufficient for your needs.

5. Higher Deductibles and Copayments: Insurance plans often require deductibles and copayments, which can add up over time. Paying out-of-pocket allows you to have more control over your therapy expenses without worrying about meeting deductibles or paying co-pays for each session.

6. Diagnosing: In order to use insurance, therapists need to prove medical necessity and must give the client a diagnosis. Some people don't like this, and would prefer to work outside of the insurance system. It's important to note that difficulties with using insurance for therapy vary depending on individual insurance plans and providers. I recommend thoroughly reviewing your insurance policy.

```
Call   the   number   on   the   back   of   your
insurance  card  to  speak  with  your  insurance
provider to understand the specific coverage
and limitations.
```

Therapy fees can vary widely depending on factors such as location, therapist experience, and specialization.

> ```
> Sliding  Scale  fees  are  another  option  of  a
> flexible  pricing  system  where  the  cost  of
> sessions is adjusted based on your ability to
> pay, often determined by your income level.
> ```

I will provide you with some average prices for individual therapy and couples therapy in the specified states.

(Please note these are just rough estimates of out-of-pocket (cash-pay) fees, and actual therapy fees may vary. It's best to contact therapists directly to inquire about their specific fees and any potential sliding scale options based on income.)

CASH PAY PRICES IN 2023

State	Individual Therapy	Couples Therapy
° California	$100-250	$150-300
° Texas	$80-200	$120-250
° New York	$150-300	$200-400
° Michigan	$80-150	$120-200
° Colorado	$80-200	$120-250
° Florida	$80-150	$120-200

Modalities You Can Choose From

Every therapist has a unique style and flavor to how they do therapy. Every therapist will feel different to talk to. Different modalities, or theories therapists use, offer a unique view on navigating life's challenges and how the process of change will be for each client.

Here is a breakdown of what each modality has to offer you.

THERAPY TYPE	DESCRIPTION
(CBT) Cognitive Behavioral Therapy	Focuses on identifying and changing negative thought patterns and behaviors to develop healthier coping strategies.
Psychodynamic Therapy	Explores unconscious processes and early life experiences to gain insight into unconscious patterns and work through unresolved conflicts.
Solution-Focused Therapy	A goal-oriented approach that focuses on finding solutions and developing practical strategies to achieve desired outcomes.
Mindfulness-Based Therapy	Incorporates mindfulness practices to cultivate present-moment awareness and reduce stress.
(DBT) Dialectical Behavior Therapy	Combines CBT with mindfulness to regulate emotions, improve interpersonal relationships, and develop coping skills.

(ACT) Acceptance and Commitment Therapy	Emphasizes accepting difficult thoughts and emotions while committing to value-aligned actions.
Gestalt Therapy	Emphasizes the present moment and holistic experience to increase self-awareness and explore unresolved emotions.
Narrative Therapy	Views individuals as authors of their own stories, focusing on deconstructing and reimagining narratives.
(EFT) Emotion-focused therapy	Helps understand and regulate emotions to improve well-being and relationships, great for couples.
Existential Therapy	Explores fundamental human existence questions, helping find purpose and meaning.
Person-Centered Therapy	Emphasizes the therapeutic relationship and unconditional positive regard, creating a non-judgmental environment.
Family Systems Therapy	Examines family unit dynamics to understand patterns and work towards healthier dynamics.
Couples Therapy	Focuses on improving communication and resolving conflicts in romantic relationships.
(EMDR) Eye movement desensitization and reprocessing	A specialized therapy for trauma, helping process traumatic memories and develop coping mechanisms.
(IFS) Internal family systems therapy	Focuses on understanding and harmonizing internal parts to promote healing and self-compassion.

Directories: The Yellow Pages of Therapists

Here are the top five online directories to help you connect with therapists who align with your needs and preferences. It can be confusing to navigate and actually find the person you are going to talk to.

Here are some sites to make it easier.

1. Psychology Today (www.psychologytoday.com)

Psychology Today is one of the most widely used directories for finding therapists. It allows you to search for therapists based on location, specialties, insurance accepted, and more. The directory provides detailed profiles of therapists, including their credentials, approach, and contact information.

2. GoodTherapy (www.goodtherapy.org)

GoodTherapy is another popular directory that connects individuals with therapists. It offers a comprehensive search feature that allows you to filter therapists based on location, specialties, and treatment approaches. GoodTherapy also provides educational resources and articles on mental health topics.

3. TherapyDen (www.therapyden.com)

TherapyDen is a directory that focuses on promoting inclusivity and diversity in therapy. It allows you to search for therapists based on location, identities, and specialties. TherapyDen also provides information about therapists' values, approaches, and fees.

4. Open Path Collective (www.openpathcollective.org)

Open Path Collective is a directory that connects individuals with affordable therapy. It offers a network of therapists who provide reduced-rate (sliding-scale) sessions if you cannot afford the full cost of therapy.

5. Zocdoc (www.zocdoc.com)

While primarily known as a platform for finding medical doctors, Zocdoc also includes a directory for therapists. It allows you to search for therapists based on location, specialties, insurance accepted, and availability. Zocdoc provides user reviews and ratings to help you make informed decisions.

6. Alma (www.helloalma.com)

Alma is a platform connects individuals with high-quality therapists based on various factors such as location, specialties, and insurance accepted. Alma emphasizes creating a personalized match between clients and therapists, providing a seamless booking process and ongoing support.

These directories offer a wide range of therapists with various specialties and treatment approaches. It's important to review therapists' profiles, read reviews, and consider your specific needs when choosing a therapist. Additionally, it's always a good idea to contact therapists directly to inquire about their availability, fees, and any other questions you may have. Plus, you usually get that free phone or video consultation.

Taking the first step to call a therapist can be challenging, especially if you're already experiencing anxiety. But remember, reaching out for help is a courageous act of self-care. By making that call, you're opening the door to a brighter future and the support you deserve. Embrace the discomfort and trust that you're taking a powerful step toward your personal growth.

This book will help you decide if you and your partner are ready to start therapy, opening the door to a new chapter as a **Different Me, Different Us.**

Motivation Follows Action.

Y'all got this!

CITATIONS

Bancroft, J., Graham, C. A., Janssen, E., & Sanders, S. A. (2009). The Dual Control Model: Current status and future directions. Journal of Sex Research, 46(2 & 3), 121-142.

Bancroft, J., & Janssen, E. (2000). The dual control model of male sexual response: A theoretical approach to centrally mediated erectile dysfunction. Neuroscience and Biobehavioral Reviews, 24(5), 571-579.

Blair, K. L., Pukall, C. F., Smith, K. B., & Cappell, J. (2014). Differential Associations of Communication and Love in Heterosexual, Lesbian, and Bisexual Women's Perceptions and Experiences of Chronic Vulvar and Pelvic Pain. Journal of Sex & Marital Therapy, 41(5), 498-524. https://doi.org/10.1080/0092623X.2014.931315

Brown, B. (2011, January 3). The power of vulnerability. [Video]. YouTube. https://youtu.be/iCvmsMzlF7o

Brown, B. (Host). (2021, March 26). Brené with Emily and Amelia Nagoski on burnout and how to complete the stress cycle (No. 31) [Audio podcast episode]. In Unlocking Us. Brené Brown.

Byra, S., & Żyta, A. (2018). Sexuality of adults with intellectual disabilities as described by support staff workers. Croation Review of Rehabiltation Research. 53. https://www.researchgate.net/publication/323383793_Sexuality_of_adults_with_intellectual_disabilities_as_described_by_support_staff_workers

Condos, D. (Host). (May 19, 2020). Dr. Peter Levine on How Trauma Changes Our Minds and Bodies (S2 No. 3) [Audio Podcast Episode]. In Beyond Theory Podcast. Meadows Behavioral Healthcare. https://beyondtheorypodcast.com/dr-peter-levine-on-how-trauma-changes-our-minds-and-bodies/

Felitti, V. J., Anda, R. F., Nordenberg, D., Williamson, D. F., Spitz, A. M., Edwards, V., Koss, M. P., & Marks, J. S. (1998). Relationship of childhood abuse and household dysfunction to many of the leading causes of death in adults:

Flück, C. E. (2023, November 13). *Ambiguous genitalia in the newborn*. Endotext [Internet]. https://www.ncbi.nlm.nih.gov/books/NBK279168/

Firml, T. [@tinafirml] (2024, February 2). *Happy Valentine's Day one and all!* [Video]. Tiktok.

Fraley, R. C., Roisman, G. I., Booth-LaForce, C., Owen, M. T., & Holland, A. S. (2013). Interpersonal and genetic origins of adult attachment styles: a longitudinal study from infancy to early adulthood. *Journal of personality and social psychology*, *104*(5), 817-838. https://doi.org/10.1037/a0031435

Gewirtz-Meydan, A., & Opuda, E. (2023). The sexual fantasies of childhood sexual abuse survivors: A rapid review. *Trauma, Violence, & Abuse*, 24(2), 441-453. https://doi.org/10.1177/15248380211030487

Grey, M. (2024). *Regarding Masturbation Awareness Month*. LinkedIn

Gottman, J., & Gottman, J. S. (2015). *The seven principles for making marriage work: A practical guide from the country's foremost relationship expert*. Harmony.

Hendrix, H., & Hunt, H. L. (2004). *Getting the love you want: A guide for couples*. New York: Henry Holt and Co.

Herzog, M. (2024, April 27). *Context: What is it + why is it important to your sex life- part I*. The Center for Modern Relationships. https://centerformodernrelationships.com/blog-list/2020/9/21/context-what-is-it-why-is-it-important-to-your-sex-life-part-i

Hili. (2023, December 6). *What the polyvagal theory is and how it works*. Sacred Path Holistic Therapy. https://sacredpathholistictherapy.com/what-the-polyvagal-theory-is-and-how-it-works/

Hundley, M. (2023) *Mending Conflict: Essential Phrases for Mending Conflicts in Relationships Attachment Theory Zine 01*. Self-Published

In-depth quiz - The blueprint breakthrough. The Blueprint Breakthrough -. (2024, April 4). https://theblueprintbreakthrough.com/

Iasenza, S. (2020). *Transforming sexual narratives: A relational approach to sex therapy*. Routledge.

Janssen, E., & Bancroft, J. (2023). The Dual Control Model of Sexual Response: A scoping review, 2009-2022. *Journal of Sex Research*, 60(7), 948-968. https://doi.org/10.1080/00224499.2023.2219247

Johnson, S. (2008). *Hold me tight: Seven conversations for a lifetime of love*. Little, Brown Spark.

Kerner, I. (2009). *She comes first: The thinking man's guide to pleasuring a woman*. William Morrow Paperbacks.

Lehmiller, J. J. (2018). *Tell me what you want: The science of sexual desire and how it can help you improve your sex life*. Robinson.

Lehmiller, J. J., & Gormezano, A. M. (2023). Sexual fantasy research: A contemporary review. *Current Opinion in Psychology*, 49, 101496. https://doi.org/10.1016/j.copsyc.2022.101496

Ley, D. J. (2018). *Ethical Porn for Dicks: A Man's Guide to Responsible Viewing Pleasure*. New York: ThreeL Media.

Maltz, W. (2002). Treating the sexual intimacy concerns of sexual abuse survivors. *Sexual and Relationship Therapy*, 17(4), 321-327. https://doi.org/10.1080/1468199021000017173

Meana, M., & Binik, Y. M. (2022). The biopsychosocial puzzle of painful sex. *Annual Review of Clinical Psychology*, 18(1), 471-495. https://doi.org/10.1146/annurev-clinpsy-072720-014549

Nagoski, E. (2015). *Come as you are: The surprising new science that will transform your sex life*. Simon & Schuster.

Nagoski, E. (2019). *Come Together: How to Cultivate Healthy Relationships Through the Science of Desire*. New York: Simon & Schuster.

Noah, T. (2022, October 19). *Men, Intimacy & the "Right to Sex" - between the scenes: The Daily Show*. [Video]. YouTube. https://youtu.be/eYmFyjy2EmQ

Norrholm, S. D., & Ressler, K. J. (2009). *Genetics of anxiety and trauma-related disorders*. Neuroscience, 164(1), 272-87. https://doi.org/10.1016/j.neuroscience.2009.06.036

Perel, E. (2006). *Mating in Captivity: Unlocking erotic intelligence*. Harper.

Perel, E. (2017). *The State of Affairs: Rethinking Infidelity*. Harper.

Real, T. (2007). *The new rules of marriage: What you need to know to make love work*. Ballantine Books.

Schnarch, D. (2009). *Passionate Marriage: Keeping love and intimacy alive in committed relationships*. W. W. Norton & Company.

Sheffer, M. (2018). *Sex Therapy: Reviewing the Issues within the Field* (thesis).

Shiels, A. (2023). *Safety, then connection: An attachment-based workbook for couples*. Self-published.

Shiels, A. [@dr._angelica_shiels]. (2024, July 1). So when my kids, who I love more than anything in the world were very young I #OCD #anxiety #intrusivethoughts [Video]. Instagram. https://www.instagram.com/reel/C85PdPivCEm/?ig_mid=A83B8DFE-9B2A-4B3B-8551-43E9818BD523&utm_source=igweb&fall_back_to_web=false&launch_app_store=true

Sobel, V., Zhu, Y.-S., & Imperato-McGinley, J. (2004). Fetal hormones and sexual differentiation. *Obstetrics and Gynecology Clinics of North America*, 31(4), 837-856. https://doi.org/10.1016/j.ogc.2004.08.005

Tatkin, S. (2012). *Wired for love: How understanding your partner's brain and attachment style can help you defuse conflict and build a secure relationship*. New Harbinger Publications.

The Adverse Childhood Experiences (ACE) Study. *American Journal of Preventive Medicine*, 14(4), 245-258. https://doi.org/10.1016/S0749-3797(98)00017-8

Tomikawa, Y. (2023, May 15). *Setting private practice rates: Average fees per session, by City*. The Couch: A Therapy & Mental Wellness Blog. https://blog.zencare.co/therapy-fees-private-practice-by-city/

UCI Health. (2023). *What you may not know about testosterone.* https://www.ucihealth.org/blog/2023/03/testosterone-facts

Uloko, M., Isabey, E. P., & Peters, B. R. (2023). How many nerve fibers innervate the human glans clitoris: A histomorphometric evaluation of the dorsal nerve of the clitoris. *The Journal of Sexual Medicine*, *20*(3), 247–252. https://doi.org/10.1093/jsxmed/qdac027

Warren, R. (2007). *The purpose driven life: What on earth am I here for?* Zondervan.

Weiss, R. (2017). *Out of the doghouse: A step-by-step relationship-saving guide for men caught cheating*. Health Communications, Inc.

Worsley, R., Santoro, N., Miller, K. K., Parish, S. J., & Davis, S. R. (2016). Hormones and female sexual dysfunction: Beyond estrogens and androgens—findings from the Fourth International Consultation on Sexual Medicine. *The Journal of Sexual Medicine*, *13*(3), 283–290. https://doi.org/10.1016/j.jsxm.2015.12.014

Journal

Made in the USA
Middletown, DE
17 August 2024